California
Science

PEARSON
Scott
Foresman

Editorial Offices: Glenview, Illinois • Parsippany, New Jersey • New York, New York
Sales Offices: Boston, Massachusetts • Duluth, Georgia • Glenview, Illinois •
Coppell, Texas • Sacramento, California • Mesa, Arizona

Series Authors

Dr. Timothy Cooney
Professor of Earth Science and Science Education
University of Northern Iowa (UNI)
Cedar Falls, Iowa

Dr. Jim Cummins
Professor
Department of Curriculum, Teaching, and Learning
University of Toronto
Toronto, Canada

Dr. James Flood
Distinguished Professor of Literacy and Language
School of Teacher Education
San Diego State University
San Diego, California

Barbara Kay Foots, M.Ed.
Science Education Consultant
Houston, Texas

Dr. M. Jenice Goldston
Associate Professor of Science Education
Department of Elementary Education Programs
University of Alabama
Tuscaloosa, Alabama

Dr. Shirley Gholston Key
Associate Professor of Science Education
Instruction and Curriculum Leadership Department
College of Education
University of Memphis
Memphis, Tennessee

Dr. Diane Lapp
Distinguished Professor of Reading and Language Arts in Teacher Education
San Diego State University
San Diego, California

Sheryl A. Mercier
Classroom Teacher
Dunlap Elementary School
Dunlap, California

Karen L. Ostlund, Ph.D.
UTeach Specialist
College of Natural Sciences
The University of Texas at Austin
Austin, Texas

Dr. Nancy Romance
Professor of Science Education & Principal Investigator
NSF/IERI Science IDEAS Project
Charles E. Schmidt College of Science
Florida Atlantic University
Boca Raton, Florida

Dr. William Tate
Chair and Professor of Education and Applied Statistics
Department of Education
Washington University
St. Louis, Missouri

Dr. Kathryn C. Thornton
Former NASA Astronaut
Professor
School of Engineering and Applied Science
University of Virginia
Charlottesville, Virginia

Dr. Leon Ukens
Professor Emeritus
Department of Physics, Astronomy, and Geosciences
Towson University
Towson, Maryland

Steve Weinberg
Consultant
Connecticut Center for Advanced Technology
East Hartford, Connecticut

Contributing Author  Content Consultants

Dr. Michael P. Klentschy
Superintendent
El Centro Elementary School
District
El Centro, California

Consulting Author

Dr. Olga Amaral
*Chair, Division of Teacher
Education*
San Diego State University
Calexico, California

Science Content Consultants

Dr. Herbert Brunkhorst
Chair
Department of Science,
Mathematics and Technology
College of Education
California State University, San
Bernardino
San Bernardino, California

Dr. Karen Kolehmainen
Department of Physics
California State University, San
Bernardino
San Bernardino, California

Dr. Stephen D. Lewis
Earth and Environmental Sciences
California State University, Fresno
Fresno, California

**Adena Williams Loston,
Ph.D.**
Chief Education Officer
Office of the Chief Education
Officer

Clifford W. Houston, Ph.D.
*Deputy Chief Education Officer for
Education Programs*
Office of the Chief Education
Officer

Frank C. Owens
Senior Policy Advisor
Office of the Chief Education
Officer

Deborah Brown Biggs
*Manager, Education Flight Projects
Office*
Space Operations Mission
Directorate, Education Lead

Erika G. Vick
*NASA Liaison to Pearson Scott
Foresman*
Education Flight Projects Office

William E. Anderson
*Partnership Manager for
Education*
Aeronautics Research Mission
Directorate

Anita Krishnamurthi
Program Planning Specialist
Space Science Education and
Outreach Program

Bonnie J. McClain
Chief of Education
Exploration Systems Mission
Directorate

Diane Clayton, Ph.D.
Program Scientist
Earth Science Education

Deborah Rivera
Strategic Alliances Manager
Office of Public Affairs
NASA Headquarters

Douglas D. Peterson
*Public Affairs Office,
Astronaut Office*
Office of Public Affairs
NASA Johnson Space Center

Nicole Cloutier
*Public Affairs Office,
Astronaut Office*
Office of Public Affairs
NASA Johnson Space Center

Reviewers

Elaine Chasse-DeMers
Teacher
Taylor Street School
Sacramento,
California

Kevin Clevenger
Teacher
Oak Chan
Elementary
Folsom, California

Kim Eddings
Teacher
Madison Elementary
Pomona, California

Joseph Frescatore
Teacher
Chavez Elementary
San Diego,
California

Candace Gibbons
Teacher
Freedom Elementary
Clovis, California

Anne Higginbotham
Teacher
Arundel Elementary
San Carlos,
California

Sean Higgins
Teacher
Monte Verde
Elementary
San Bruno,
California

Sharon Janulaw
Science Education
Specialist
Sonoma County
Office of Education
Santa Rosa,
California

Jeanne E. Martin
Teacher
John Gill School
Redwood City,
California

Mark Allen Schultz
Teacher
Theodore Judah
Elementary
Folsom, California

Corinne Schwartz
Teacher
Lincrest Elementary
Yuba City,
California

Schelly T. Solko
Teacher
Loudon School
Bakersfield,
California

Bobbie Stumbaugh
Teacher
Roy Cloud School
Redwood City,
California

Kimberly Thiesen
Teacher
Freedom Elementary
Clovis, California

Carole Bialek Vargas
Teacher
Empire Oaks
Elementary
Folsom, California

Bonita J. Walker-Davis
Teacher
Don Riggio School
Stockton, California

Debra Willsie
Teacher
Tarpey Elementary
Clovis, California

Olivia Winslow
Teacher
Earl Warren
Elementary
Sacramento,
California

California Science

How do forces cause objects to move?

Chapter 2 • Sound

How is sound made?

Why do plants and animals look the way they do?

How do animals grow and change?

Chapter 5 • All About Plants

How do plants grow and change?

What are some of Earth's natural resources?

Chapter 6 • Rocks and Soil

Chapter 7 • Fossils and Dinosaurs

How can people learn about Earth long ago?

Science Process Skills

Observe

A scientist who wants to find out more about fossils and dinosaurs observes many things. You use your senses to find out about things too.

Classify

Scientists classify fossils and dinosaurs. You classify when you sort or group things by their properties.

Estimate and Measure

Scientists build models of dinosaurs to learn more about them. First scientists make a careful guess about the size of a dinosaur. Then they measure each fossil as they build a skeleton.

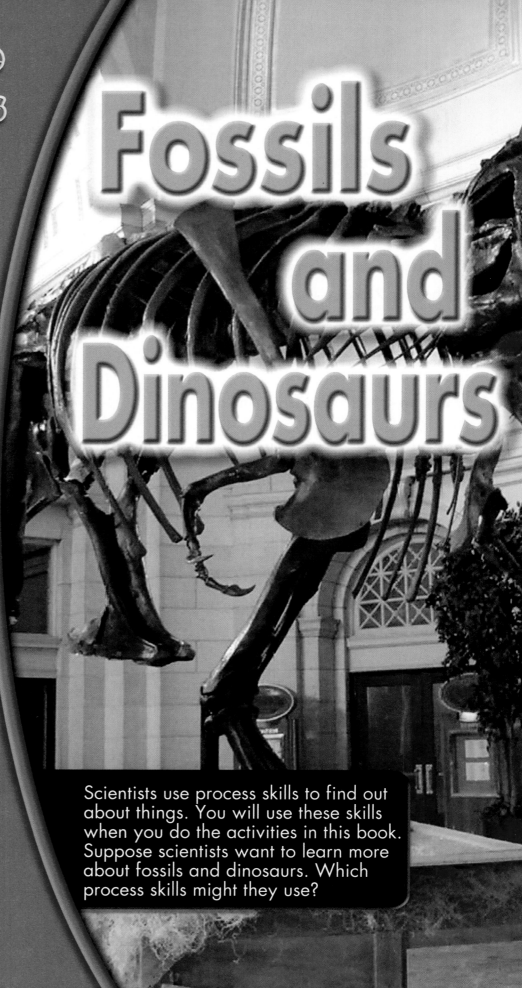

Fossils and Dinosaurs

Scientists use process skills to find out about things. You will use these skills when you do the activities in this book. Suppose scientists want to learn more about fossils and dinosaurs. Which process skills might they use?

Infer

Scientists are always learning about fossils and dinosaurs. Scientists draw a conclusion or make a guess from what they already know.

Predict

First scientists tell what they think will happen. Then they do an experiment.

Make and Use Models

Scientists might make and use models of dinosaurs. Models show what scientists already know.

Science Process Skills

Investigate and Experiment

Scientists plan and do an investigation as they study fossils and dinosaurs.

Make Hypotheses

Think of a question you have about fossils and dinosaurs. Make a statement that you can test to answer your question.

Control Variables

Scientists plan a fair test. Scientists change only one thing in their test. Scientists keep everything else the same.

Suppose you were a scientist. You might want to learn more about fossils and dinosaurs. What questions might you have? How would you use process skills to help you learn?

Collect Data

Scientists record what they observe and measure. Scientists put this data into charts or graphs.

Interpret Data

Scientists use what they learn to solve problems or answer questions.

Communicate

Scientists tell what they learn about fossils and dinosaurs.

Using Scientific Methods for Science Inquiry

Scientific methods are ways of finding answers. Scientific methods have these steps. Sometimes scientists do the steps in a different order. Scientists do not always do all of the steps.

Ask a question.

Ask a question that you want answered.

How does sunlight affect the way plants grow?

Make your hypothesis.

Tell what you think the answer is to your question.

If a plant is moved away from sunlight, then the plant will grow toward sunlight.

Plan a fair test.

Change only one thing.

Keep everything else the same.

Move one plant away from the window.

Do your test.

Test your hypothesis. Do your test more than once. See if your results are the same.

Collect and record your data.

Keep records of what you find out. Use words or drawings to help.

Tell your conclusion.

Observe the results of your test. Decide if your hypothesis is right or wrong. Tell what you decide.

Plants will grow toward sunlight.

Go further.

Use what you learn. Think of new questions or better ways to do a test.

Ask a Question

Make Your Hypothesis

Plan a Fair Test

Do Your Test

Collect and Record Your Data

Tell Your Conclusion

Go Further

Science Tools

Scientists use many different kinds of tools.

Safety goggles
You can use safety goggles to protect your eyes.

Magnifier
A magnifier makes objects look larger.

Balance
A balance is used to measure the weight of objects. Most scientists measure weight in grams or kilograms.

Graduated cup
You can use a graduated cup to measure liquid.

Magnet
You can use a magnet to see if an object is made of certain metals.

Meterstick
You can use a meterstick to measure how long something is. Scientists use a meterstick to measure in meters.

Thermometer
A thermometer measures temperature. Most thermometers have Celsius and Fahrenheit scales. Most scientists use the Celsius scale.

Metric Ruler
You can use a metric ruler to measure how long something is. Scientists use a metric ruler to measure in centimeters and millimeters.

Microscope
A microscope helps you see things that are too small to see with your eyes.

Safety

Safety in the Classroom

You need to be careful when doing science activities. These pages include safety tips to remember:

- Listen to your teacher.
- Read each activity carefully.
- Never taste or smell materials unless your teacher tells you to.
- Wear safety goggles when needed.
- Handle scissors and other equipment carefully.
- Keep your work place neat and clean.
- Clean up spills right away.

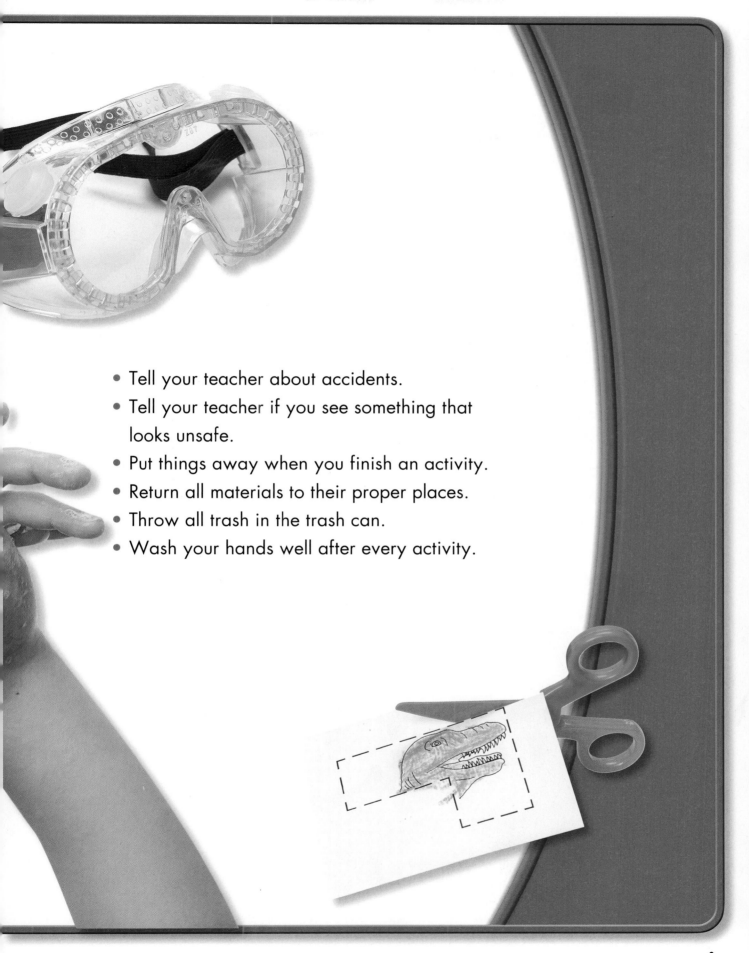

- Tell your teacher about accidents.
- Tell your teacher if you see something that looks unsafe.
- Put things away when you finish an activity.
- Return all materials to their proper places.
- Throw all trash in the trash can.
- Wash your hands well after every activity.

Safety

Safety at Home

Safety Tips

- Put toys, shoes, and books away. Do not leave anything lying on the floor.
- Do not play with sharp objects such as knives.
- Wash your hands with soap and warm water before eating.
- Clean up all spills right away.
- Do not run indoors or jump down stairs.

Fire Safety Tips

- Never use matches or lighters.
- Never use the stove or oven without the help of an adult.
- Get out quickly if your home is on fire.
- Stop, drop, and roll if your clothing catches on fire. Do not run.
- Know two ways to get out of your home.
- Practice fire escape routes with your family.

Electrical Safety Tips

- Do not touch electrical outlets.
- Use the plug to pull out an electrical cord. Do not pull the cord.
- Keep all electrical objects away from water.

Earthquake Tips

- Make a plan with an adult about what to do if there is an earthquake.
- Get under or lie next to a heavy table, desk, or piece of furniture.
- Stay away from glass doors and windows.
- Help your family make an earthquake kit. Put water, food, a flashlight, and a radio in your kit.

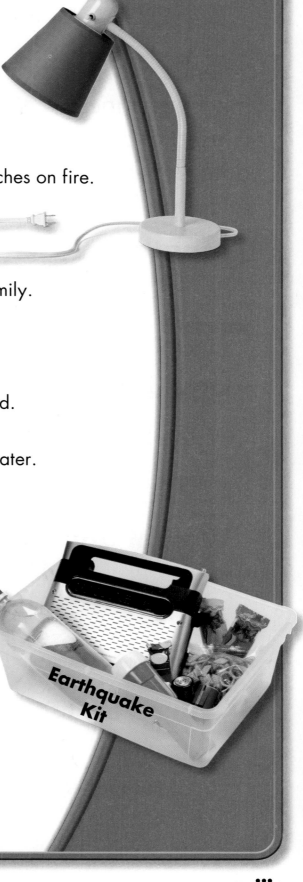

Earthquake Kit

Metric and Customary Measurement

Science uses the metric system to measure things. Metric measurement is used around the world. Here is how different metric measurements compare to customary measurements.

• Length and Distance

meter

foot

One meter is longer than 3 feet.

• Liquid Volume

cup

liter

One liter is greater than 4 cups.

• Weight and Mass

1 pound

1 kilogram

One kilogram is greater than one pound.

• Temperature

Fahrenheit

Celsius

Water freezes at 0°C and 32°F.

CALIFORNIA

Unit A

Physical Sciences

California Field Trip
California State Fair

Sacramento, California

The California State Fair is in Sacramento. The fair has taken place for more than 150 years. You can learn about farming in California when you visit the fair. You can see how farmers use tools and machines.

Find Out More

Research to find out more about the California State Fair.

- Make a book of pictures that shows what happens at the fair. Write a sentence about each picture.

- Make your own display for the fair. Tell your class all about it.

Sacramento

CALIFORNIA Standards Focus Questions

- How can you describe position?
- What is motion?
- What is friction?
- How can tools and machines make things move?
- What is gravity?
- What are magnets?

Chapter 1

Forces and Motion

How do forces cause objects to move?

force

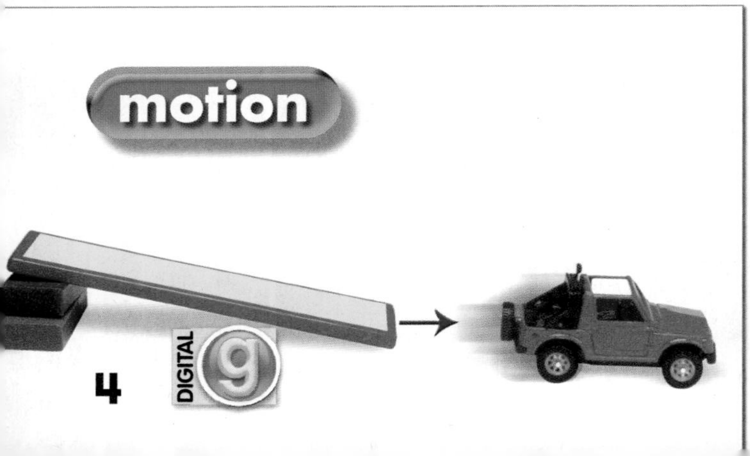

motion

friction

4

Chapter 1 Vocabulary

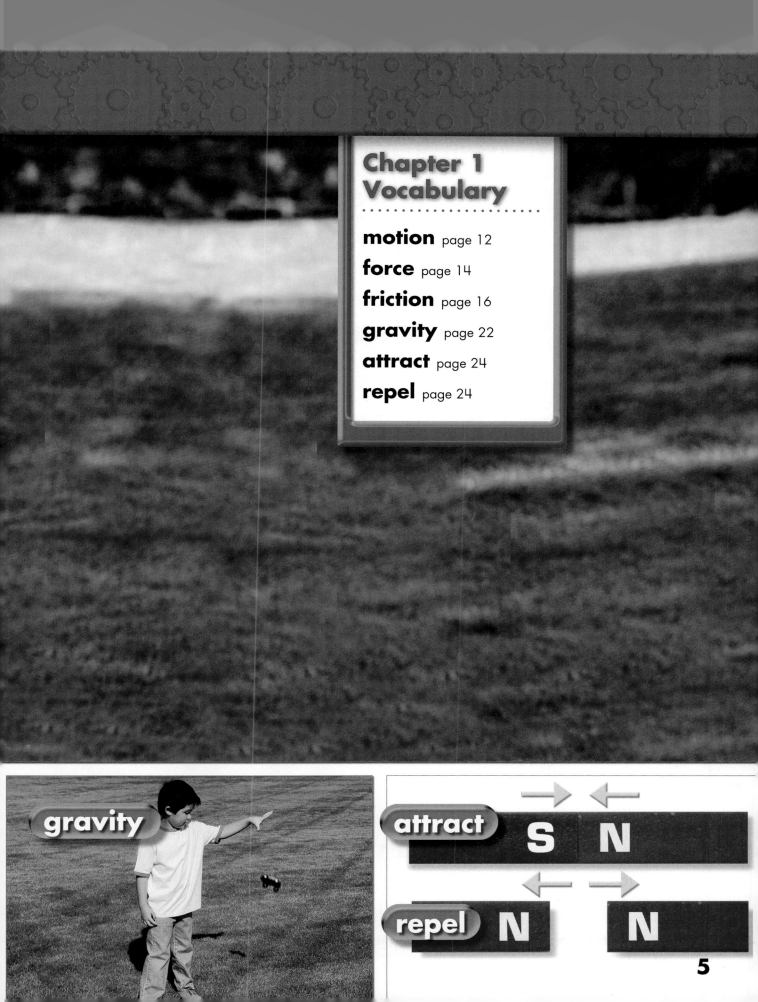

gravity

attract **S** **N**

repel **N** **N**

5

Explore Where are the objects?

Materials

coin

eraser

crayon

paper clip

tape

cardboard

What to Do

1 Get a coin, eraser, crayon, and paper clip.

2 Tape the objects where your teacher tells you.

3 **Observe** where the objects are.

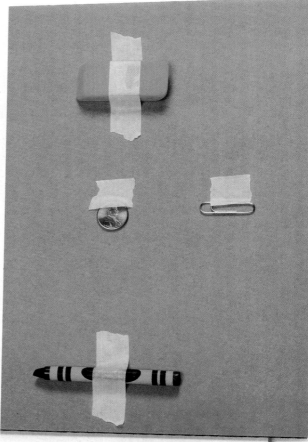

Process Skills

Sometimes you are given oral instructions. **Observe** your work to check for mistakes.

Explain Your Results

Observe Tell if an object is above, below, or to the right of the coin.

DIGITAL Lab zone

TARGET SKILL

Cause and Effect

A **cause** is why something happens.
An **effect** is what happens.

Science Story

Faster and Farther

The girl is pushing a toy car. She causes the toy car to move faster when she pushes it harder. She causes the toy car to travel farther when she pushes it harder.

Apply It!

Observe Push a book across your desk. Stop pushing. What happens?

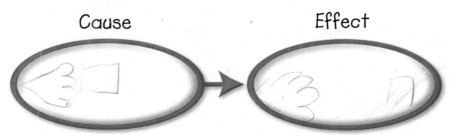

Cause   Effect

Use Some Force!

Sung to the tune of "If You're Happy"
Lyrics by Gerri Brioso & Richard Freitas/The Dovetail Group, Inc.

If you want to move the ball, use some force.

If you want to move the ball, use some force.

If you want it to go far, kick it hard and there you are.

You just moved the ball by using lots of force.

Lesson 1

How can you describe position?

It's time to play soccer! Look at the picture of the man and the boy. You can see that the soccer ball is in front of the boy. The man is behind the boy.

You can use words like *in front of* and *behind* to help you describe the position of something. Position is where an object is.

You can also use the words *left* and *right* to help you describe position. Look at the picture below. You can use an object that does not move to tell where the coach is. The goal does not move. The coach is to the right of the goal.

You can also use things in the background to help you tell where something is. The trees are in the background. The soccer field is in front of the trees.

You can measure to find out how far away the soccer ball is from the goal. You measure distance using meters and centimeters. The soccer ball is about 5 meters away from the goal.

✓ **Lesson Review**

1. What words can help you describe position?

2. **Writing in Science** Write a sentence. Describe where the bench is.

Lesson 2

What is motion?

Motion is the act of moving. Different things move in different ways. Some things can move in a straight line. Other things can move back and forth or around and around.

The speed and direction of motion can be changed. Push on the pedals of a bicycle. You change speed. Turn the handlebars, and you change direction.

Look at the picture. The car and bicycle started from the same place. They started at the same time. The bicycle has traveled for one minute. The car has traveled for one minute. Is the car or the bicycle closer to the library?

The car traveled farther than the bicycle. The car traveled faster than the bicycle.

Measuring Motion

Look for Active Art animations at www.pearsonsuccessnet.com

You can measure how far something moves. Roll a toy truck down from the top of a ramp. Record how far it rolls. Make the ramp higher. Record how far the truck rolls from the top. When did the truck roll farther?

1. ✓ Checkpoint What is motion?

2. **Cause and Effect** Why is the car closer to the library than the bicycle is?

TARGET SKILL

LIBRARY

Force

A push or pull that can make something move is called a **force.** A force changes the way an object moves.

An object will not start moving unless it is given a push or a pull. An object will move in the direction it is pushed or pulled.

A moving object does not need any force to keep it moving. A moving object that is pushed or pulled will speed up, slow down, or change direction.

How can you make a soccer ball roll just a little bit? How can you make it roll farther? It depends on how much force you use. Tap a soccer ball gently. It will not move far.

Tap!

Kick the soccer ball harder.
It will move farther.
It takes more force to
move objects farther.

It also takes more force to
move heavier objects than
lighter objects. Would you
need more force to move
a book or a desk?

Bam!

✓ Lesson Review

1. What is force?

2. ✏ **Writing in Science** How
can the amount of force used
change how far an object
will move?

DIGITAL
NSTA
SciLinks
keyword:
force
code:
gr2p14

What is friction?

Think about kicking a ball across a field. Why would the ball stop moving? **Friction** is a force. Friction makes a moving object slow down or stop moving. The friction between the ball and the grass slows the ball down.

Look at the bicycles in these pictures. A bicycle will move faster on a smooth road than it will on grass. The friction between the bicycle tires and the grass will make the bicycle slow down.

✓ Lesson Review

1. How does friction change the motion of an object?

2. **Cause and Effect** What causes a bicycle to move more slowly on grass than on a smooth road?

How can tools and machines make things move?

Tools and machines use pushes and pulls to help us move things. Tools and machines help us do things we can not do alone.

A hit or push by a baseball bat will change the direction of a pitched ball.

A hammer is a tool. A hammer will move a nail into a piece of wood.

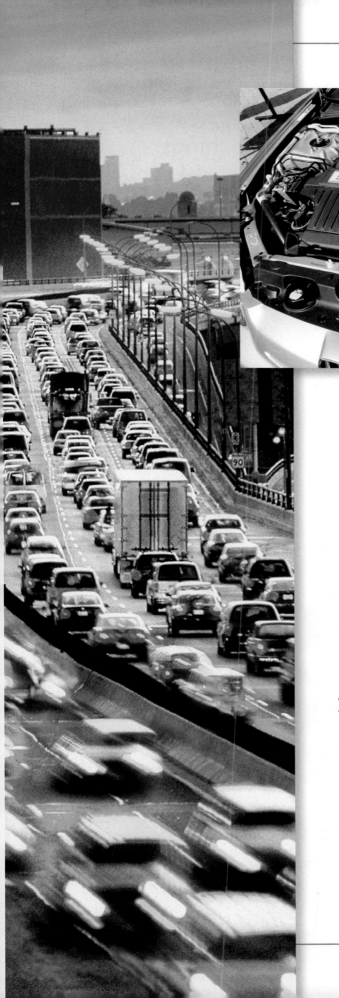

A car is a machine. The engine of a car uses force to make the wheels go around. This force causes the car to move.

1. ✓Checkpoint How do tools and machines help us?

2. How does a hammer help you do something you could not do alone?

Using Tools and Machines

Tools and machines make it easier to move things. A shovel is a tool. A shovel can help move sand, dirt, or rocks.

A wagon is a machine. You can use a wagon to move heavy things. You can use a wagon to move many things at one time.

✔️ Lesson Review

1. Suppose you need to move a heavy box. What could you use to help you move it?

2. Writing in Science Tell how you can use tools and machines at home.

What is gravity?

Gravity is a pulling force. Gravity pulls things toward the center of Earth. Look at the girl jumping in the air. She will not float up. Gravity will pull her down.

Look at the boy dropping the toy. What will happen to the toy? Gravity will pull it down.

How much something weighs tells how strong the pull of gravity is on it. A car weighs more than a baseball weighs. The pull of gravity is stronger on the car than on the baseball.

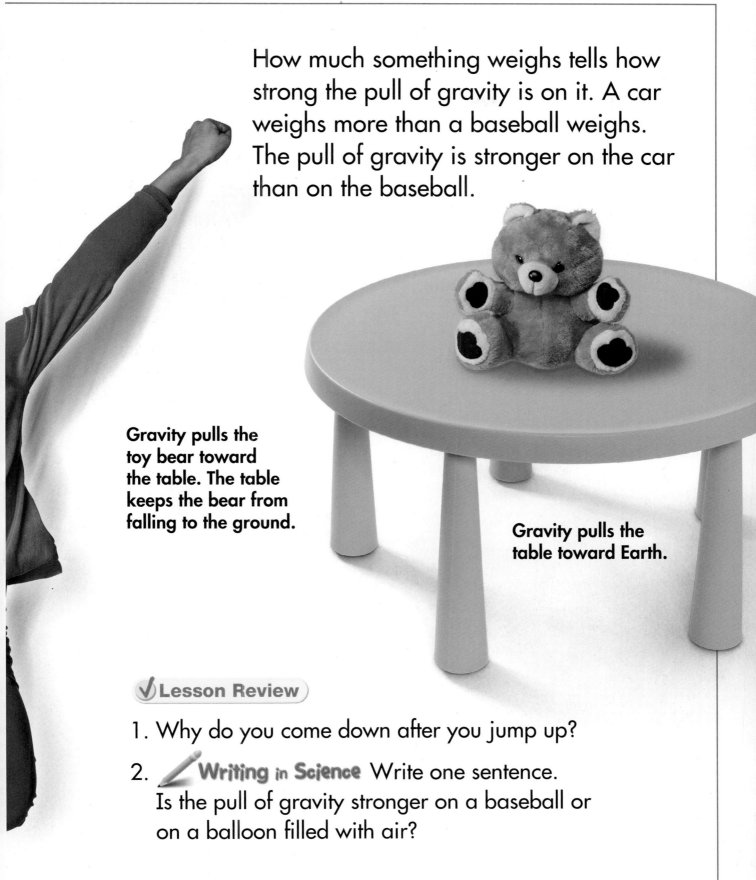

Gravity pulls the toy bear toward the table. The table keeps the bear from falling to the ground.

Gravity pulls the table toward Earth.

✓ Lesson Review

1. Why do you come down after you jump up?

2. ✏ Writing in Science Write one sentence. Is the pull of gravity stronger on a baseball or on a balloon filled with air?

Lesson 6

What are magnets?

Magnets can pull certain metal objects. We say magnets attract these objects. **Attract** means to pull toward. Magnets can attract or repel other magnets. **Repel** means to push away.

This magnet has attracted several metal objects.

Magnets have poles. A pole is the place on a magnet that has the strongest push or pull. Look at the poles of these magnets. The N stands for north pole. The S stands for south pole.

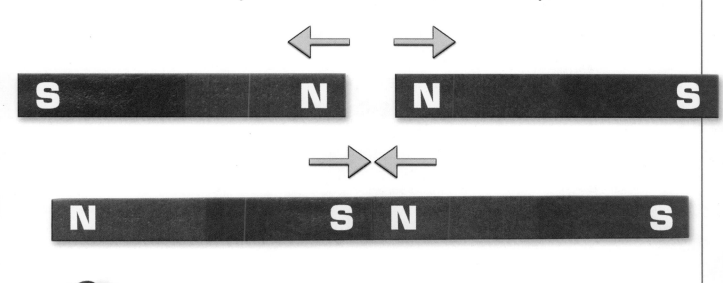

Put like poles together. They repel each other. Put opposite poles together. They attract each other.

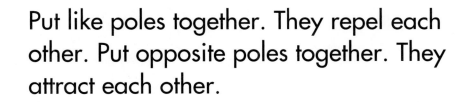

1. ✓Checkpoint When do magnets attract each other?

2. **Cause and Effect** What causes one magnet to repel another magnet?

How Magnets Move Objects

A magnet can move some things without touching them. Look at the picture below. The spoon is moving toward the magnet. The magnet is not touching the spoon. The force of the magnet pulls the spoon.

The magnet attracts the metal on the spoon.

Patterns Made by a Magnet

Sprinkle tiny pieces of iron on a piece of paper. Move a magnet under the piece of paper. Watch the pieces of iron move. Look for a pattern.

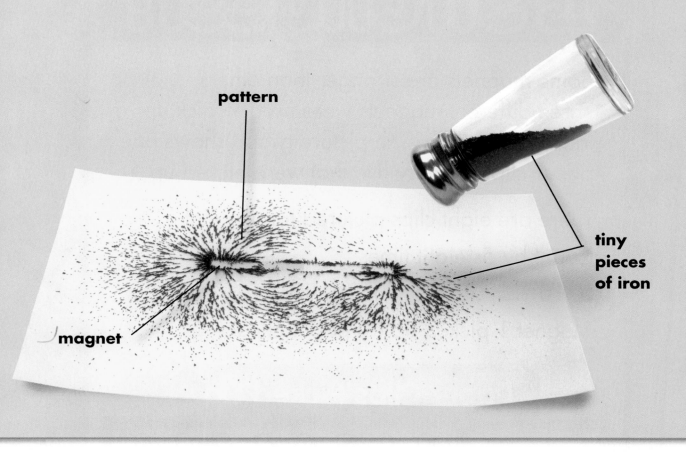

pattern

tiny pieces of iron

magnet

✔ **Lesson Review**

1. What can happen if you put a magnet near an object made of metal?

2. ✏ **Writing in Science** Try to pick up different objects using a magnet. Write about what happens.

Which Magnet Is Strongest?

Some magnets are stronger than others. Three different magnets were used to pick up large paper clips. The picture graph shows one paper clip for every five that were picked up.

There are eight clips pictured for Magnet 1.

Count by 5s eight times:

5, 10, 15, 20, 25, 30, 35, 40

Magnet 1 picked up 40 paper clips.

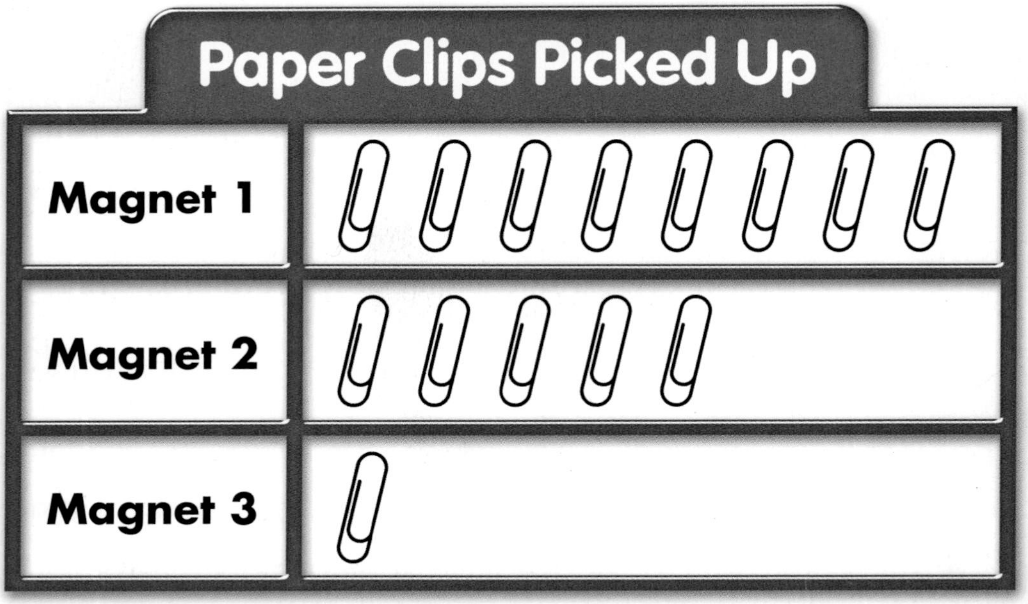

Paper Clips Picked Up

Magnet 1	𝅉 𝅉 𝅉 𝅉 𝅉 𝅉 𝅉 𝅉
Magnet 2	𝅉 𝅉 𝅉 𝅉 𝅉
Magnet 3	𝅉

Each 𝅉 = 5 paper clips

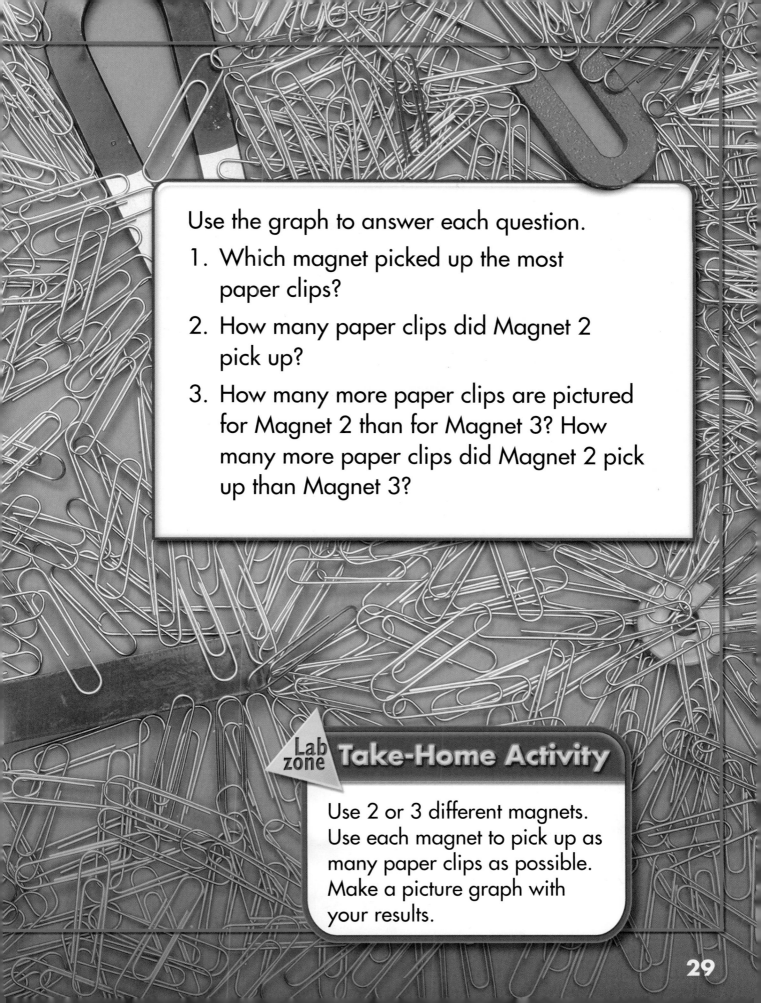

Use the graph to answer each question.

1. Which magnet picked up the most paper clips?

2. How many paper clips did Magnet 2 pick up?

3. How many more paper clips are pictured for Magnet 2 than for Magnet 3? How many more paper clips did Magnet 2 pick up than Magnet 3?

Lab zone **Take-Home Activity**

Use 2 or 3 different magnets. Use each magnet to pick up as many paper clips as possible. Make a picture graph with your results.

Investigate Can a magnet move an object without touching the object?

Materials

magnet

paper clip

screw

construction paper

What to Do

1 Can a magnet move a paper clip? Find out.

2 Can a magnet move a paper clip with paper in between them? Find out.

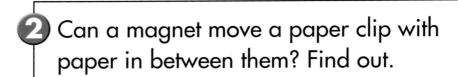

3 Can a magnet move a paper clip with a tabletop in between them? Find out.

4 **Predict** What would happen if you used a screw, not a paper clip? Repeat steps 1 to 3.

	Observation	Prediction	Observation
	Did the paper clip move? (yes or no)	**Will the screw move?** (yes or no)	**Did the screw move?** (yes or no)
Magnet Only			
Magnet and Paper			
Magnet and Tabletop			

Explain Your Results

Think about your **observations.** Can a magnet move an object without touching it? Explain.

Go Further

Can magnets pull objects through a piece of foil? Make a plan to find out.

Focus on the BIG Idea

Forces cause objects to move by pushing or pulling. The speed and direction of motion can be changed by using force.

Lesson 1

How can you describe position?
- Words such as *above*, *in front of*, *behind*, *left*, and *right* describe the position of an object.

Lesson 2

What is motion?
- Motion is the act of moving.
- A force is a push or a pull.

Lesson 3

What is friction?
- Friction is a pull that makes a moving object slow down or stop.

Lesson 4

How can tools and machines make things move?
- Tools and machines use pushes and pulls to make things move.

Lesson 5

What is gravity?
- Gravity is a force that pulls things toward Earth.

Lesson 6

What are magnets?
- Magnets can move some objects without touching them.

Cross-Curricular Links

English–Language Arts

Building Vocabulary

Look at pages 4 and 5. Find the words *gravity* and *friction*. Write three sentences about each word. Read your sentences. Revise your sentences to give more details.

Mathematics

Comparing Distance

Suppose you push a book across the floor. The book moves 36 cm. Push again using more force. The book moves 56 cm. Write a number sentence. How much farther did the book move the second time?

History–Social Science

Isaac Newton and Gravity

Isaac Newton was a person who made a difference. Use the library-media center to learn about Isaac Newton. What did he teach us about gravity?

Challenge!

English–Language Arts

Poles of a Magnet

How can you find the poles of a magnet that is not a bar magnet? Make a plan to find out. Write sentences that tell what you learned. Organize your ideas before you write.

Vocabulary

Which picture goes with each word?

1. force (page 14)

2. friction (page 16)

3. gravity (page 22)

4. attract (page 24)

5. repel (page 24)

Think About It

6. What force keeps objects from floating in the air? (page 22)

7. What are two things about motion that can change? (page 12)

8. ✏ Writing in Science Tell how you might use a tool or machine to move a pile of rocks. (pages 20–21)

9. Process Skills Observe Drop a crayon. Describe what happens. (pages 22–23)

10. TARGET SKILL Cause and Effect What would happen if you placed a bar magnet near a paper clip? (pages 24–27)

Cause   Effect

California Standards Practice

Write the letter of the correct answer.

11. What is motion?

  A the force that pulls objects to Earth

  B the force that makes objects slow down or stop

  C a strong push or pull

  D the act of moving

12. The picture shows a girl kicking a soccer ball. How can you describe the position of the woman in the picture?

  A in front of the girl

  B to the left of the ball

  C behind the girl

  D in front of the ball

Exercising in Space

Read Together

Playing ball and riding a bike are exercises. They use motion and force. Gravity helps you exercise on Earth. You push against the force of gravity when you lift your arms.

Suppose you were on the Space Shuttle. You would not feel the tug of gravity. Instead, you would float around the cabin! This makes exercising in space harder than on Earth.

Astronauts have to wear weights on the treadmill used in space.

The cycle machine exercises the heart, legs, and arms.

Astronauts in space need exercise. Astronauts use special exercise machines in space. One machine is like a rowing machine. It pushes and pulls on muscles. Astronauts are strapped on each machine so they don't float away!

Lab zone **Take-Home Activity**

Draw a picture of an exercise machine that you could use in space. Show how it will help exercise your bones and muscles. Include straps so you don't float away.

NASA

Meet Luther Jenkins

Read Together

Luther Jenkins works at NASA. He is an aerospace engineer. He studies airplanes and spacecraft. Math and science were Luther's favorite subjects in school. At first, Luther wanted to become a lawyer. He soon discovered that he likes to learn how things work. He decided to become an engineer.

At NASA, Luther uses math and science in his work. He uses wind tunnels to conduct experiments on airplanes and spacecraft. He works with special tools to measure the speed of air.

Lab zone Take-Home Activity

Research to learn about the airplane flown by the Wright brothers in 1903. Draw a picture of their airplane.

CALIFORNIA
Standards Focus Questions

- What is sound?
- What is volume?
- What is pitch?

Chapter 2

Sound

How is sound made?

vibrate

volume

pitch

Explore How can you change the sound made by a vibrating object?

Be careful!

Wear safety goggles.

Materials

safety goggles

plastic ruler

What to Do

 Push down on one end of the ruler. Let go. **Observe** What do you hear?

Hold this end down.

15 cm

2 Slide the ruler back. Push down on the ruler again. Observe.

Explain Your Results

Observe How did the sound change when you moved the ruler back? **Predict** How will the sound change if you move the ruler forward?

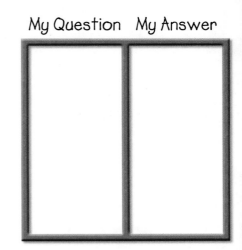

TARGET SKILL

Ask and Answer Questions

Good readers **ask and answer** questions as they read. *How, why, when,* and *what if* are words that often begin a question.

Science Article

Drums

Instruments can make high sounds or low sounds. Large drums, such as kettle drums, make a low sound. Smaller drums, such as bongo drums, make a higher sound than a kettle drum.

Apply It!

Observe Read the article and look at the picture. Use the chart to help you **ask and answer** a question.

My Question	My Answer

You Are There

Listen to the Sounds!

Sung to the tune of "Bicycle Built For Two"
Lyrics by Gerri Brioso & Richard Freitas/The Dovetail Group, Inc.

Soft sounds, loud sounds,
High sounds and some low.
Listen for sounds all around you
Everywhere that you may go.

Lesson 1

What is sound?

Look at the picture. What musical instruments do you see? Each instrument makes a different sound.

Sound is made when an object vibrates. **Vibrate** means to move quickly back and forth.

A vibrating object makes the air around it vibrate. You hear the sound when the vibrations reach your ear.

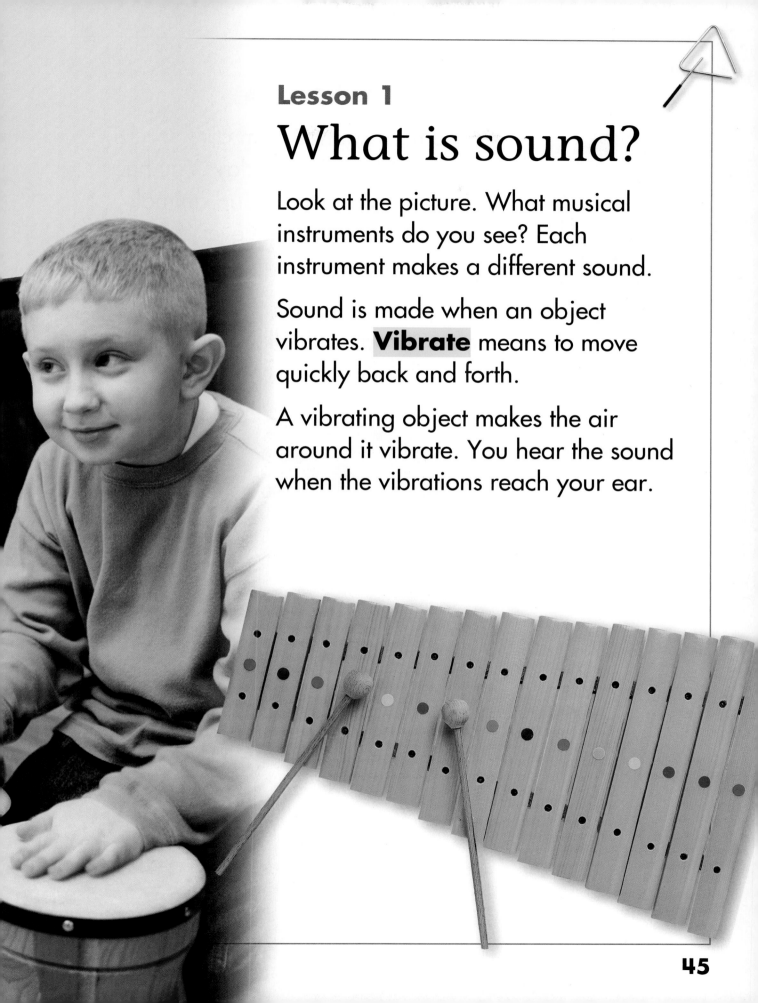

Different Sounds

You hear sounds from cars, trucks, and airplanes every day. You hear sounds from people and animals too. Vibrations make every sound you hear.

Put your fingers on the front of your throat and talk. You will feel the vibration.

Parts of your throat vibrate when you talk.

Animals make sounds too. A cricket makes sounds by rubbing one wing on the other wing. Then the other wing vibrates to make sound.

Look at the pictures to see how other animals make sounds.

The rattlesnake makes sounds by vibrating the rattle in its tail.

Zebras make sounds by vibrating parts of their throat, lips, and nose.

✔ Lesson Review

1. How is sound made?

2. **Ask and Answer Questions** Think of how an animal makes sounds. Ask a question about it. Then answer your question.

Lesson 2

What is volume?

One way to describe sound is by its volume.
Volume means how loud or soft a sound is.

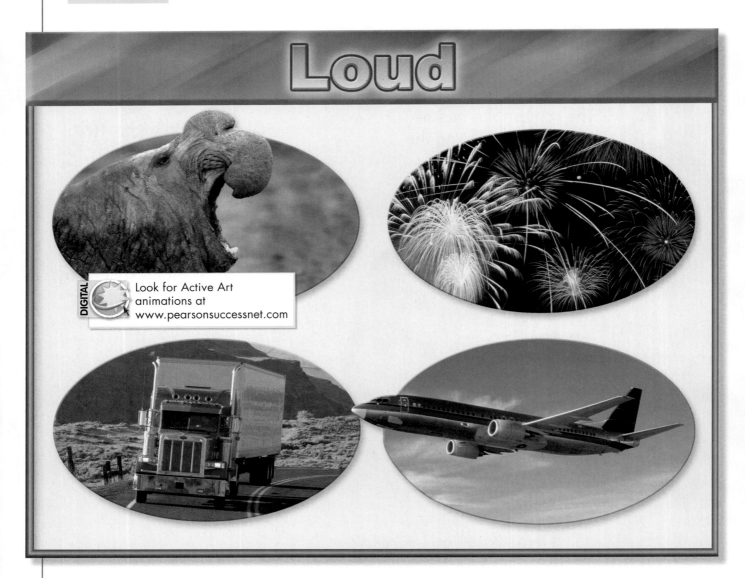

Loud

Look for Active Art
animations at
www.pearsonsuccessnet.com

Think about an airplane. It makes a loud sound.
The pictures on this page show things that can
make loud sounds.

Think about a falling leaf. It makes a soft sound. The pictures on this page show things that can make soft sounds.

Soft

✓ Lesson Review

TARGET SKILL

1. How does volume describe sound?

2. **Ask and Answer Questions** Think about how you can make loud and soft sounds. Ask a question. Then answer the question.

49

Lesson 3
What is pitch?

A triangle makes a sound with a high pitch.

Pitch is another way to describe sound. **Pitch** means how high or low a sound is. Objects that vibrate quickly make a sound with a high pitch. Objects that vibrate slowly make a sound with a low pitch.

This snare drum makes a sound with a lower pitch than the triangle.

This boy is playing the violin. The short, thin strings vibrate quickly.

Look at the instruments. The strings on the violin will make sounds with a high pitch. The strings on the double bass will make sounds with a lower pitch than the snare drum.

This girl is holding a double bass. The long, thick strings vibrate slowly.

✓ Lesson Review

1. How does pitch describe sound?

2. ✎ **Writing in Science** What does pitch tell you about the way an object vibrates?

DIGITAL NSTA SciLinks keyword: **Pitch** code: gr2p50

Measuring Sounds

This bar graph compares the volume of some sounds. A vacuum cleaner is much louder than a whisper.

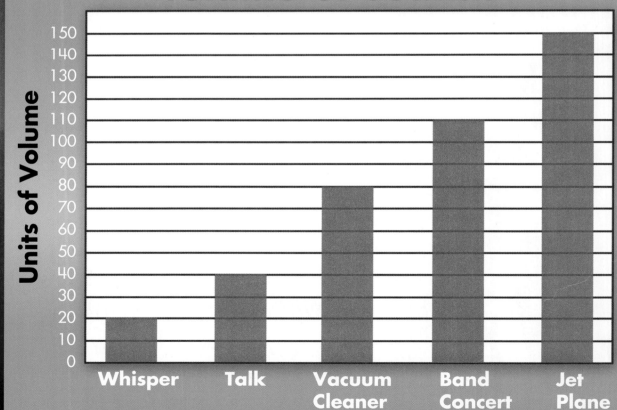

Volume of Sounds

Units of Volume

Kinds of Sound	Volume
Whisper	20
Talk	40
Vacuum Cleaner	80
Band Concert	110
Jet Plane	150

Kinds of Sound

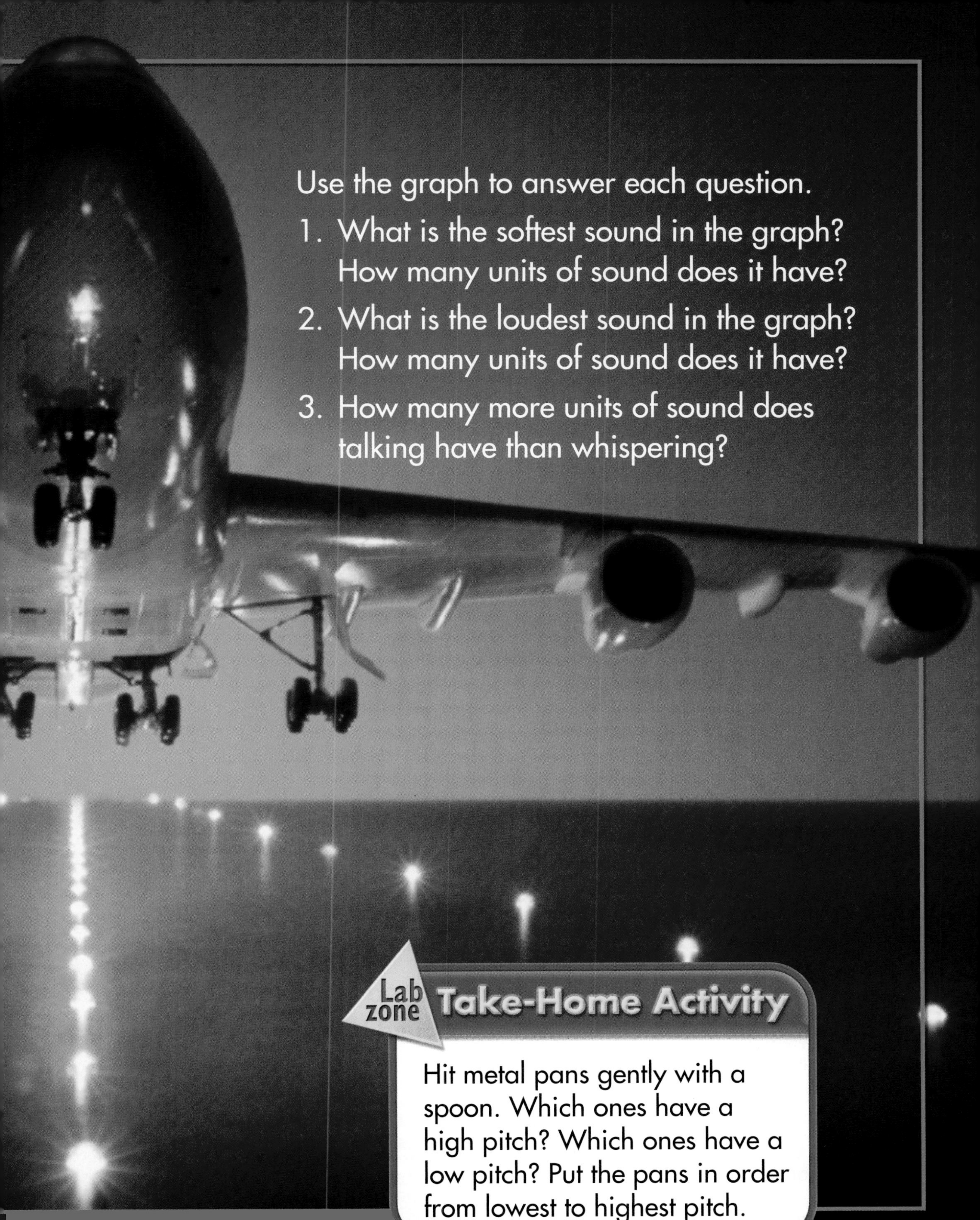

Use the graph to answer each question.

1. What is the softest sound in the graph? How many units of sound does it have?

2. What is the loudest sound in the graph? How many units of sound does it have?

3. How many more units of sound does talking have than whispering?

Lab zone **Take-Home Activity**

Hit metal pans gently with a spoon. Which ones have a high pitch? Which ones have a low pitch? Put the pans in order from lowest to highest pitch.

Investigate How can you change sound?

Materials

safety goggles

rubber band

tissue box

2 pencils
(unsharpened)

What to Do

1 Put the rubber band around the box. Put 2 pencils under the rubber band.

Be careful!

Wear your goggles.

2 Pluck the rubber band hard. Then pluck gently.

Process Skills

Before you **predict**, look for a pattern. A pattern can help you make a good prediction.

3 Fill in the chart. Tell how the sound changed.

Is the sound loud or soft?

Plucks	Sound (loud or soft)
Hard plucks	
Gentle plucks	

DIGITAL

Lab zone

4 Move the pencils far apart. Pluck.
Is the sound high or low? Record.

5 Move the pencils close together.
Predict. Will the sound be high or low?
Pluck. Record.

Is the sound high or low?

Pencils	Sound (high or low)
Far apart	
Close together	

Explain Your Results

1. What made the sound high?
   What made the sound loud?
2. **Predict** What would make a
   soft, low sound? Find out.

Go Further

Listen to the sound from
a tuning fork, drum,
and stringed instrument.
Touch different parts.
Think about what you
feel and what you hear.

Focus on the BIG Idea

All sounds are caused by vibration. Sounds can be loud or soft. Sounds can have a high or a low pitch.

Lesson 1

What is sound?
- Sound is made when an object vibrates.
- Vibrate means to move quickly back and forth.

Lesson 2

What is volume?
- One way to describe sound is by its volume.
- Volume is how loud or soft a sound is.

Lesson 3

What is pitch?
- Pitch is how high or low a sound is.
- Objects that vibrate quickly make sounds with a high pitch.
- Objects that vibrate slowly make sounds with a low pitch.

Cross-Curricular Links

English–Language Arts

Building Vocabulary

Look again at pages 40 and 41. Write a story about a time when you were at a game or a concert that was very loud. Describe the event, and tell why it was loud. Use the vocabulary words *volume* and *pitch* in your story.

Mathematics

Number of Strings

Pressing keys on a piano makes strings vibrate. There are 52 white keys and 36 black keys. How many keys are there in all? How many more white keys are there than black keys?

Visual and Performing Arts

The Sounds that Animals Make

Draw a picture of an animal that is making a sound. Color your picture. Write a sentence that tells about the sound.

Challenge!

English–Language Arts

Loud Sounds and Soft Sounds

Use a thesaurus to find other words that describe loud sounds and soft sounds. Write a sentence using the words that you find.

Vocabulary

Which picture goes with each word?

1. vibrate (page 45)

2. volume (page 48)

3. pitch (page 50)

Think About It

4. Why does a violin make a sound with a higher pitch than a double bass? (pages 50–51)

5. What happens when vibrations reach your ear? (page 45)

6. ✎ Writing in Science Name two different instruments. Tell about the pitch of each instrument. (pages 50–51)

7. Process Skills Observe Look around your school. Tell about some things that make loud sounds and some things that make soft sounds. (page 43)

8. 🎯 Ask and Answer Questions Think about what you have learned about pitch and volume. Ask a question. Then answer the question. (pages 48–51)

My question

My answer

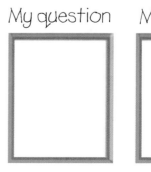

California Standards Practice

Write the letter of the correct answer.

9. Which instrument makes the sound with the lowest pitch?

    A snare drum

    B violin

    C triangle

    D double bass

10. The picture shows a violin. What causes the sound the violin makes?

    A vibration

    B pitch

    C volume

    D air

Alejandro Purgue

Dr. Purgue is an animal scientist.

Read Together

Alejandro Purgue studies animals and the sounds they make. People and many animals make sounds using vocal cords in their throats.

While Dr. Purgue was studying bullfrogs, he made an amazing discovery. Bullfrogs actually make most of their sound through their ears!

Like other animals, bullfrogs also use their ears for hearing. Think about this amazing fact the next time you hear a frog **ribbit!**

Lab zone Take-Home Activity

Go outside at home and listen to the sounds around you. Make a list of the sounds you hear. Write *soft* or *loud* next to each sound.

Unit A Summary

Chapter 1

How do forces cause objects to move?

- Changing the amount of force used on an object changes how far and how fast the object moves.
- The force of gravity pulls objects toward Earth.
- Magnets can push or pull some metal objects.

Chapter 2

How is sound made?

- Sound is made when an object vibrates.
- Volume means how loud or soft a sound is.
- Pitch means how high or low a sound is.

Experiment How can you make a marble move farther?

Materials

2 marbles

6 books

2 metric rulers

meterstick

Ask a question.

Does the height of a ramp affect how far a marble moves?

Make a hypothesis.

How does the height of a ramp affect the speed and distance a marble will travel?

Plan a fair test.

Use the same size books and marbles.

Do your test.

1 Make 2 ramps.

4 books

2 books

Process Skills

You **collect data** when you use a chart to record your **observations.**

2 Roll a marble down each ruler.
Roll the marbles at the same time. **Observe.**

3 **Measure** how far the marbles go.
Use centimeters or meters.

Collect and record data.
Fill in the chart.

Ramp	Distance Moved (meters or centimeters)
Marble from low ramp	
Marble from high ramp	

Tell your conclusion.
How does the height of a ramp
affect how far a marble will travel?

Predict What will happen if a
ramp is 3 books high? Find out.

Go Further
Suppose the marbles
hit a wall. How would
their direction change?
Make a plan to find out.

Make Sounds with Different Pitches

- Use two plastic bottles exactly alike.

- Measure and pour 250 mL of water into one bottle.

- Measure and pour 125 mL of water into the other bottle.

- Blow across each bottle.

- Listen to the sound each bottle makes.

- Ask your classmates to tell which bottle makes the sound with the higher pitch.

Write a Fable

A fable is a story that is made up to teach a lesson. Write a fable that teaches a lesson about why everything that goes up must come down.

Read More About Physical Sciences!

Look for other books about Physical Sciences in your library-media center. One book you may want to read is:

How Do You Lift a Lion? by Robert E. Wells

This book shows how to use machines to move all kinds of fun, interesting things.

Science Fair Projects

Using Scientific Methods

1. Ask a question.
2. Make a hypothesis.
3. Plan a fair test.
4. Do your test.
5. Collect and record data.
6. Tell your conclusion.
7. Go further.

Idea 1

Changing Speed

Plan a project. Find out how different sizes of wheels affect how fast toy cars can go.

Idea 2

Listening to Sound

Plan a project. Find out how pitch changes on a musical instrument.

Unit A California Standards Practice

Write the letter of the correct answer.

1. **How can a tool or machine help you move a heavy object?**

   A by dropping it

   B by vibrating it

   C by pushing or pulling it

   D by letting it stay at rest

2. **How could you describe your position if you were standing outside?**

   A I am below the sky.

   B I am above the sky.

   C I am below the ground.

   D I am behind the ground.

3. **How could you kick a soccer ball to make it travel faster and farther?**

   A I could use less force.

   B I could use friction.

   C I could use more force.

   D I could make it stop.

4. **How are magnets used?**

   A to make objects move without touching them

   B to make sound

   C to describe position

   D to measure how far an object moves

Unit A California Standards Practice

5. **The picture shows a child dropping a toy. What will happen to the toy?**

   A It will float up.
   B Gravity will pull it to the ground.
   C Friction will pull it to the ground.
   D It will vibrate.

6. **How is sound made?**

   A by touching your throat
   B by changing volume
   C by changing pitch
   D by vibrating objects

7. **What type of sound is made when an object vibrates quickly?**

   A a loud sound
   B a sound with a low pitch
   C a sound with a high pitch
   D a soft sound

8. **How does volume describe sound?**

   A what is making a sound
   B where a sound comes from
   C how high or low a sound is
   D how loud or soft a sound is

Life Sciences

Palomar Mountain
State Park

San Diego County, California

Welcome to Palomar Mountain State Park! Palomar Mountain State Park has many kinds of trees. There are pine, cedar, fir, and oak trees. Many animals live in Palomar Mountain State Park. You might see mule deer, bobcats, gray foxes, coyotes, or mountain lions.

Find Out More

- Research to find a state park near your home.
- Find out about the plants and animals that live there.
- Write about what you learned.

Palomar Mountain State Park

CALIFORNIA
Standards
Focus Questions

- How are plants and animals like their parents?
- How does the environment affect plants and animals?
- How are plants different?
- How are animals different?

Chapter 3
Plants and Animals in Their Environment

Why do plants and animals look the way they do?

offspring

environment

inherit

Explore How do baby animals look like their parents?

Materials

Animal Pictures

crayons or markers (optional)

What to Do

1 Observe Match a baby with its parent.

You can color the animals!

2 Match other babies with their parents.

Process Skills

You use your eyes to **observe.**

Explain Your Results

Observe How are the babies like their parents? How are they different?

TARGET SKILL Use Text Features

You can **use text features** like the table of contents to help you read. Each chapter in this book has lessons. The lesson titles tell you what you will be learning about.

Science Text Feature

Table of Contents

Apply It!

Observe What will you learn about in Chapter 5? Use the graphic organizer to help you.

All About Plants

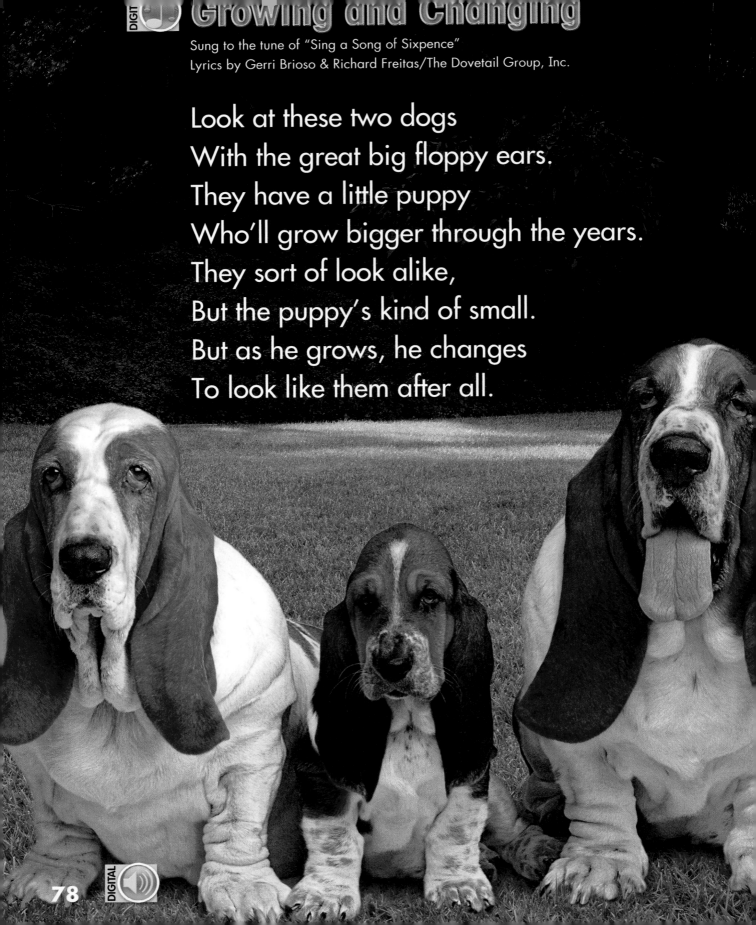

Growing and Changing

Sung to the tune of "Sing a Song of Sixpence"
Lyrics by Gerri Brioso & Richard Freitas/The Dovetail Group, Inc.

Look at these two dogs
With the great big floppy ears.
They have a little puppy
Who'll grow bigger through the years.
They sort of look alike,
But the puppy's kind of small.
But as he grows, he changes
To look like them after all.

Lesson 1

How are plants and animals like their parents?

Living things have offspring. **Offspring** are young plants and animals. Offspring look like their parents in some ways. How does the puppy in the picture look like its parents?

Oak trees always drop acorns. Each acorn may grow into a new oak tree. The young tree can grow to look like the parent tree.

Young Animals and Their Parents

Young animals can look like their parents. Offspring **inherit**, or get, some things from their parents.

Young rabbits inherit long ears, large eyes, and short tails from their parents. Young rabbits look like each other in some ways too. They may have some of the same colors in their fur or be about the same size.

The adult rabbits have different colors in their fur than their young.

Look for Active Art animations at www.pearsonsuccessnet.com

DIGITAL

Offspring may look different in some ways. How are the chicks different from each other?

The rooster and hen are the parents of these chicks. The chicks are covered with fuzzy down feathers. The feathers will change as the chicks grow. Soon the chicks will look more like their parents.

1. ✓Checkpoint What do the young rabbits inherit from their parents?

2. How are the chicks in the picture alike? How are they different?

Young Plants and Their Parents

Young plants inherit things from their parents too. Young plants are usually like the parent plant in color and shape.

The saguaro cactus is one kind of plant. The young saguaro has the same color as an adult. The young cactus does not have the same shape as the adult. The young cactus will grow arms when it is older.

A young saguaro cactus does not have arms.

These plants are called foxgloves. Very young foxglove plants do not have flowers. They will grow flowers after they are one year old. They will begin to look more like the parent plant.

You will learn how air, water, and soil can change how a plant grows in the next lesson.

✓ **Lesson Review**

1. Tell how young saguaro are like their parents.

2. **Use Text Features** Read the lesson title on page 84. What do you think this lesson will be about?

The flowers on these foxgloves are different colors.

This young foxglove does not have flowers yet.

How does the environment affect plants and animals?

The environment can change how a plant grows. The **environment** is everything around a living thing. The environment includes air, sunlight, water, and soil.

The amount of sunlight can change the way a plant looks and grows. A lily will grow more flowers in sunlight than in shade.

A lily will grow flowers in sunlight or in shade.

A mule deer in summer.

A mule deer in winter.

The environment can cause some animals to change the way they look. A mule deer's fur changes color in the winter. This makes it harder for other animals to see the deer. The deer can protect itself from other animals.

 **Lesson Review**

1. How can the environment change the way lilies look and grow?

2. **Use Text Features** Look at the table of contents in this book. How many lessons are in this chapter?

TARGET
SKILL

How are plants different?

There are many different kinds of plants. Some plants have flowers. Roses are one kind of plant that has flowers. There are many different kinds of roses. The picture below shows one kind of rose.

These roses grow on a fence. These roses come in many colors.

Roses do not all look alike. Some roses have small flowers and short stems. Other roses have large flowers and long stems. But, they are all roses!

✓ Lesson Review

1. What are some ways roses can be different?

2. ✎ **Writing in Science** Describe some kinds of flowers you have seen. Tell about the colors and sizes of the flowers.

How are animals different?

There are many different kinds of animals. Dogs are one kind of animal. There are many different kinds of dogs. Look at the picture below. It shows a family of dogs. These dogs are called terriers. There are many kinds of terriers.

These puppies have the same parents. How are the puppies alike? How are they different?

Terriers do not all look alike.
Some terriers are very large.
Other terriers are small. Their
fur can be different colors.
Some terriers have long fur.
Other terriers have short fur.

**A Scottish terrier is a
small terrier.**

**The Airedale terrier is
the largest terrier.**

✔ Lesson Review

1. What are some ways terriers are different?

2. ✏ **Writing in Science** Think about a dog you know. Find out what kind of dog it is. Describe the dog.

Charting Favorite Animals

Carlos asked each classmate to choose a favorite wild animal. He made a tally chart to record each person's answer.

Look at the tally chart. Answer the questions.

Our Favorite Animals

Animals	Number
Lions	|||
Elephants	卌 ||
Giraffes	卌 卌 卌
Bears	卌

1. How many students chose elephants?

2. Compare the number of students that chose bears to the number that chose giraffes. Use <,>, or =.

3. How many students in all answered Carlos's question? Show how you found your answer.

Lab zone Take-Home Activity

Ask your friends or family members to choose their favorite kind of flower. Make a tally chart to record the results.

Investigate What are some ways shells can vary?

Materials

5 labeled shells
(prepared by teacher)

metric ruler

magnifier

What to Do

1 **Observe** the shells.
Use a magnifier.
Compare.

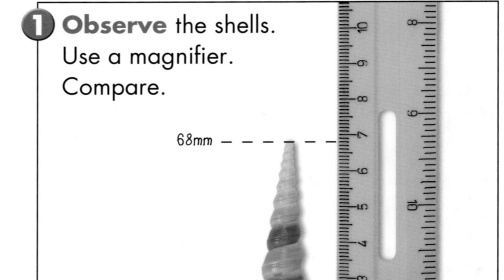

68mm

A

2 **Measure** the length of the shells.
Record.

	Shell A	Shell B	Shell C	Shell D	Shell E
Length (mm)					

3 Make a bar graph. Label each axis.

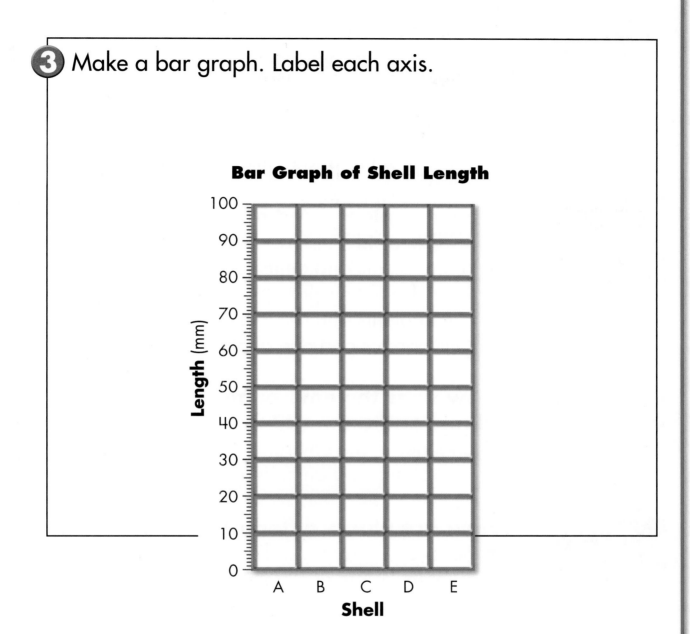

Bar Graph of Shell Length

Explain Your Results

Interpret Data Which bar was tallest? Which shell was longest?

Go Further

Sort your shells based on two or more differences such as size, shape, texture, color, and weight.

Focus on the BIG Idea

Plants and animals inherit some things from their parents that help them look the way they do. The environment also can affect the way plants and animals look and grow.

Lesson 1

How are plants and animals like their parents?

- Young plants and animals inherit some things from their parents.
- Young plants and animals may look like their parents and one another.

Lesson 2

How does the environment affect plants and animals?

- Changes in the environment can change the way plants and animals look and grow.

Lesson 3

How are plants different?

- Plants of the same kind may be different colors or different sizes.

Lesson 4

How are animals different?

- Animals of the same kind may be different colors or different sizes.

Cross-Curricular Links

English–Language Arts

Building Vocabulary

Look again at pages 74 and 75. Find the pictures for the words *offspring* and *inherit.* Write sentences about the ways offspring look like their parents. Tell some things that offspring can inherit. Read your sentences.

Mathematics

Comparing Sizes

A Scottish terrier is about 25 cm tall. An Airedale terrier is about 58 cm tall. How much taller is an Airedale terrier than a Scottish terrier?

History–Social Science

Mule Deer in California

Use a California atlas. Find out where mule deer live in California. Write about the best type of environment for a mule deer.

Challenge!

English–Language Arts

Different Kinds of Dogs

You learned about different kinds of terriers. Find out about another kind of dog, poodles. Write about different kinds of poodles. Tell how they are different from each other. Revise your paragraph. Include more details.

Vocabulary

Which picture goes with each word?

1. offspring (page 79)

2. environment (page 84)

Think About It

3. How can sunlight affect lilies? (page 84)

4. What do young rabbits inherit from their parents? (pages 80—81)

5. ✏ **Writing in Science** Tell how the environment is important to the safety of a mule deer. (page 85)

6. **Process Skills** **Observe** Look at the puppies. How are they alike and different? (pages 88—89)

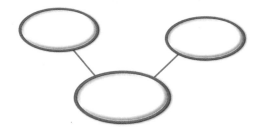

7. **TARGET SKILL** **Use Text Features** Look at the table of contents. What is this book about? (page 77)

California Standards Practice

Write the letter of the correct answer.

8. How is the young saguaro different from the parent saguaro?

   A The young saguaro does not have arms.

   B The young saguaro has arms.

   C The young saguaro has more flowers.

   D The young saguaro takes in more water.

9. Look at the picture. How will the baby chicks change?

   A The chicks will look less like their parents.

   B The chicks will look exactly like each other.

   C The chicks will all be the same color.

   D The chicks will look more like their parents.

Botanist

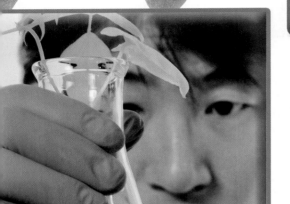

Read Together

A botanist is a person who studies plants. Botanists have many jobs. Some botanists study how the environment affects the way plants grow. For example, they study how plants grow in sunlight and in shade.

The work that botanists do helps to improve the way we use plants for food, medicine, and other things. Their research helps other people take care of our forests, wilderness areas, and parks.

Lab zone Take-Home Activity

Tell what job you would like to do if you were a botanist. Tell your family about how your job would help others.

Chapter 4

Animal Life Cycles

CALIFORNIA
Standards Focus Questions

- What is a life cycle?
- What is the life cycle of a frog?
- What is the life cycle of a mouse?
- What is the life cycle of a butterfly?
- What is the life cycle of a grasshopper?

How do animals grow and change?

life cycle

tadpole

amphibian

mammal

DIGITAL
9

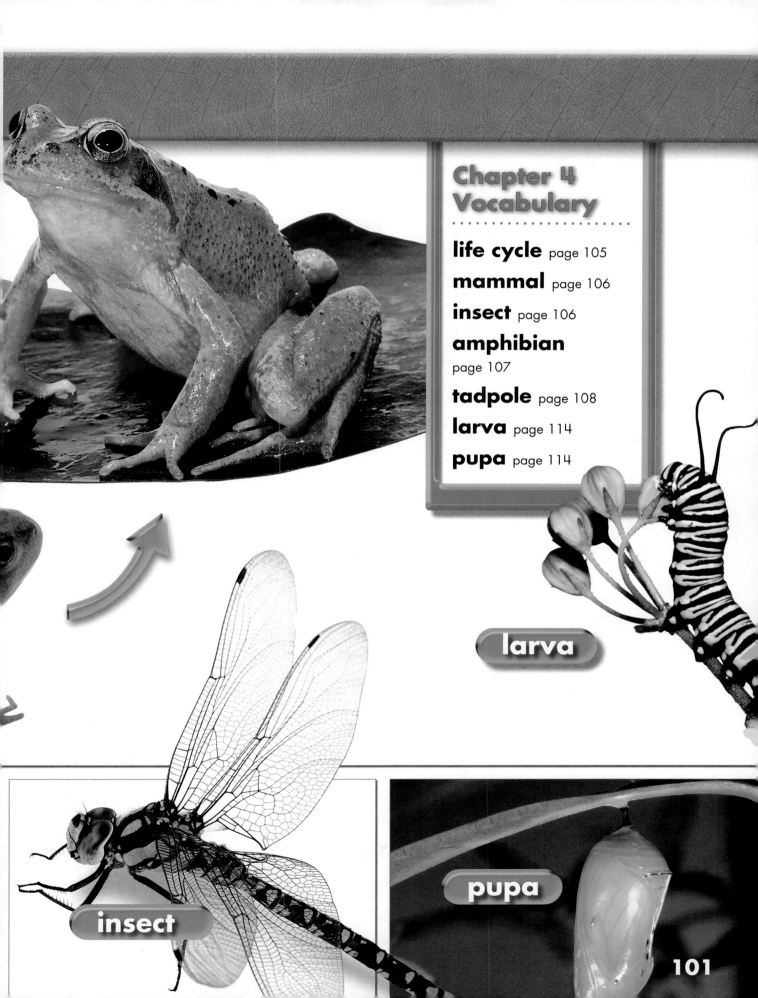

Chapter 4 Vocabulary

larva

insect

pupa

Explore What are the stages of a butterfly's life cycle?

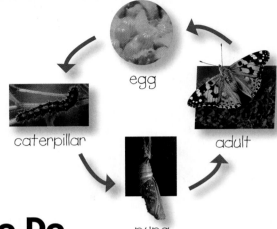

egg

caterpillar

adult

pupa

Materials

caterpillars and magnifier

butterfly habitat

crayons or markers

What to Do

1 **Observe** your caterpillars with a magnifier for 3 weeks. **Collect data.**

> Monday
> The caterpillars are little. They don't move a lot.
>
> Tuesday
> They look the same. They move a lot. They are eating.

2 Draw and write how the caterpillars changed.

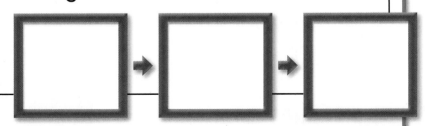

Explain Your Results

Infer What happens during the pupa stage?

How to Read Science

State the Purpose

Setting a purpose for reading will help you understand what you read. You can **state the purpose** by writing one thing you might learn about a topic. As you read, look for details that support this topic.

Before reading the science story, write one thing you might learn about a butterfly.

Science Story

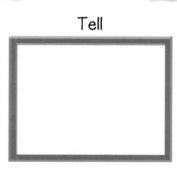

Life Cycle of a Butterfly

A butterfly grows and changes. A butterfly begins life as an egg. The egg becomes a larva called a caterpillar. The caterpillar becomes a pupa. The pupa becomes an adult butterfly.

Apply It!

Infer Tell what you think the writer wanted you to learn from the science story.

Tell

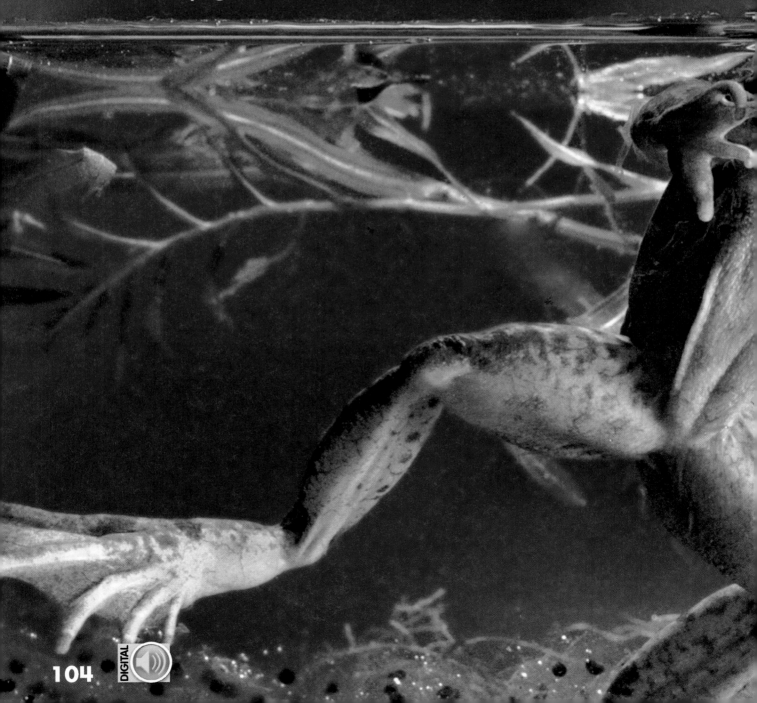

You Are There

That's a Life Cycle

Sung to the tune of "Pop Goes the Weasel"
Lyrics by Gerri Brioso & Richard Freitas/The Dovetail Group, Inc.

Let's play a game of "First, Next, and Last"
So all of us will know,
How things change before our eyes
As they grow and grow.

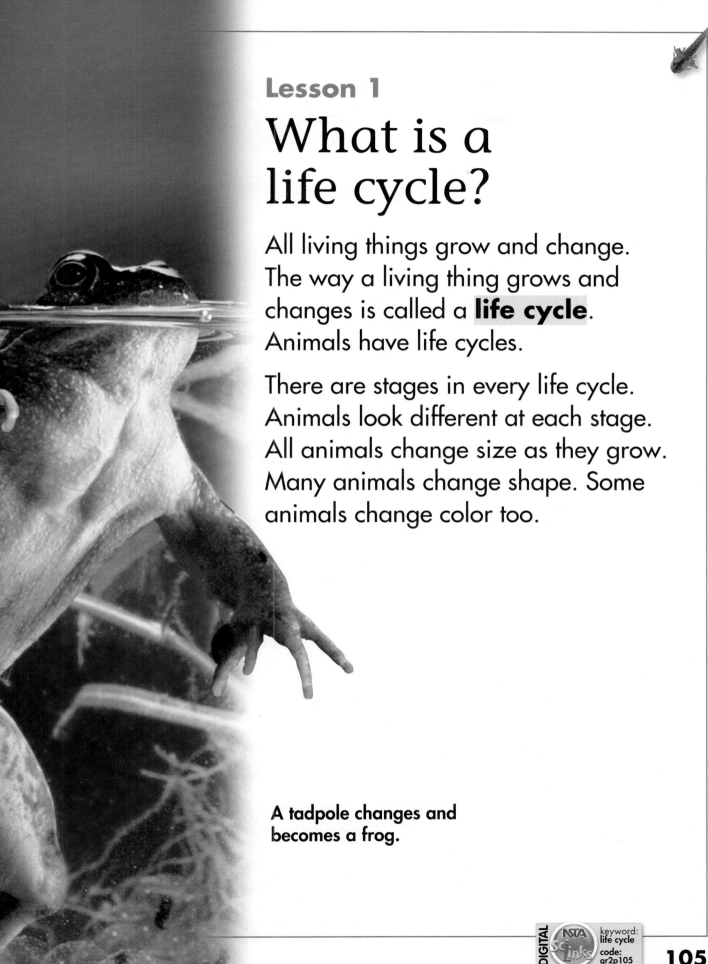

Lesson 1

What is a life cycle?

All living things grow and change. The way a living thing grows and changes is called a **life cycle**. Animals have life cycles.

There are stages in every life cycle. Animals look different at each stage. All animals change size as they grow. Many animals change shape. Some animals change color too.

A tadpole changes and becomes a frog.

Growing and Changing in Different Ways

Life cycles are different for different animals. A **mammal** is an animal that usually has hair or fur on its body. Young mammals look like their parents in many ways. Mammals change size as they get older. Some young mammals change color as they grow.

An **insect** is an animal that has three body parts and six legs. Many young insects do not look like their parents. Many young insects change size, shape, and color.

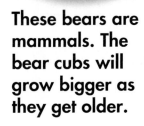

These bears are mammals. The bear cubs will grow bigger as they get older.

An **amphibian** is an animal that lives part of its life in the water. It lives part of its life on land too. Very young amphibians do not look like their parents. Young amphibians change size, shape, and color as they grow.

A toad is an amphibian.

A dragonfly is an insect. The young dragonfly looks different from the adult dragonfly.

✓ Lesson Review

1. Which kind of young animal looks like its parents in many ways?

2. **State the Purpose** Read this lesson again. What did you learn about the ways animals grow and change?

TARGET SKILL

What is the life cycle of a frog?

A frog egg is tiny. The egg feels like jelly.

A frog is an amphibian. A frog's life cycle starts with an egg. Some frog eggs float in water. The frog egg hatches. A tadpole swims out! A **tadpole** is a very young frog.

The tadpole grows and changes. The tadpole's back legs grow first. Later the tadpole's front legs will grow.

A tadpole has a tail. A tadpole begins life in water.

This tadpole is nine weeks old. Its front legs have begun to grow.

The young frog in the picture is still growing. Its legs are getting stronger. Its tail is getting smaller.

This young frog is becoming more like its parents.

1. ✓Checkpoint How does a young frog change as it grows?

2. What is the first stage in the life cycle of a frog?

From Young Frog to Adult Frog

The young frog grows into an adult frog. The adult frog may lay eggs in the water. The life cycle begins again.

DIGITAL

Look for Active Art animations at www.pearsonsuccessnet.com

An egg

A tadpole after it hatches

Young frog at twelve weeks old

An adult frog does not have a tail. An adult frog can live on land or in the water.

✓ Lesson Review

1. What are the stages in the life cycle of a frog?

TARGET SKILL

2. **State the Purpose** Look at the title of this lesson on page 108. What does the title tell you about the purpose of this lesson?

What is the life cycle of a mouse?

A mouse is a mammal. A mouse is called a mouse when it is born. A very young mouse looks like its parents, but it does not have hair!

Mice are very tiny when they are born. Their eyes are closed at birth.

The young mouse goes outside the nest when it is about two weeks old.

The mouse grows and grows. It looks more and more like its parents. An adult mouse can have baby mice of its own. The life cycle begins again.

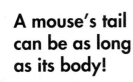

A mouse's tail can be as long as its body!

✓ **Lesson Review**

1. How does a very young mouse look different from its parents?

2. ✎ **Writing in Science** Write two sentences. Tell how a mouse changes as it grows.

What is the life cycle of a butterfly?

Some insects have four stages in their life cycle. A butterfly is an insect with four stages in its life cycle. The first stage is the egg.

The next stage is the larva. A larva hatches from the egg. A **larva** is a young insect. The butterfly larva is called a caterpillar.

A hard covering forms around the caterpillar. The caterpillar is now becoming a **pupa**. Wings begin to grow in the pupa stage.

A butterfly begins as an egg.

The caterpillar eats and grows.

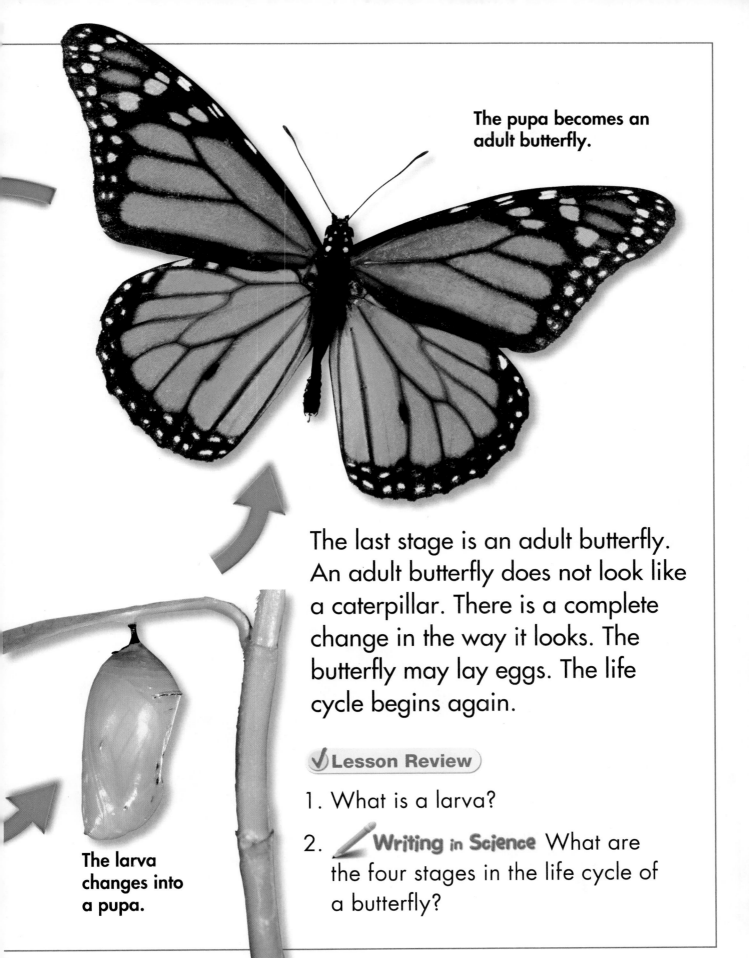

The pupa becomes an adult butterfly.

The larva changes into a pupa.

The last stage is an adult butterfly. An adult butterfly does not look like a caterpillar. There is a complete change in the way it looks. The butterfly may lay eggs. The life cycle begins again.

✓ Lesson Review

1. What is a larva?

2. ✎ **Writing in Science** What are the four stages in the life cycle of a butterfly?

What is the life cycle of a grasshopper?

A grasshopper is an insect that has three stages in its life cycle. The first stage is an egg.

The grasshopper egg hatches. The young grasshopper is called a nymph. The nymph has a hard outside covering. A nymph sheds this covering many times.

Grasshopper eggs

A nymph looks like a tiny adult.
It does not have wings.

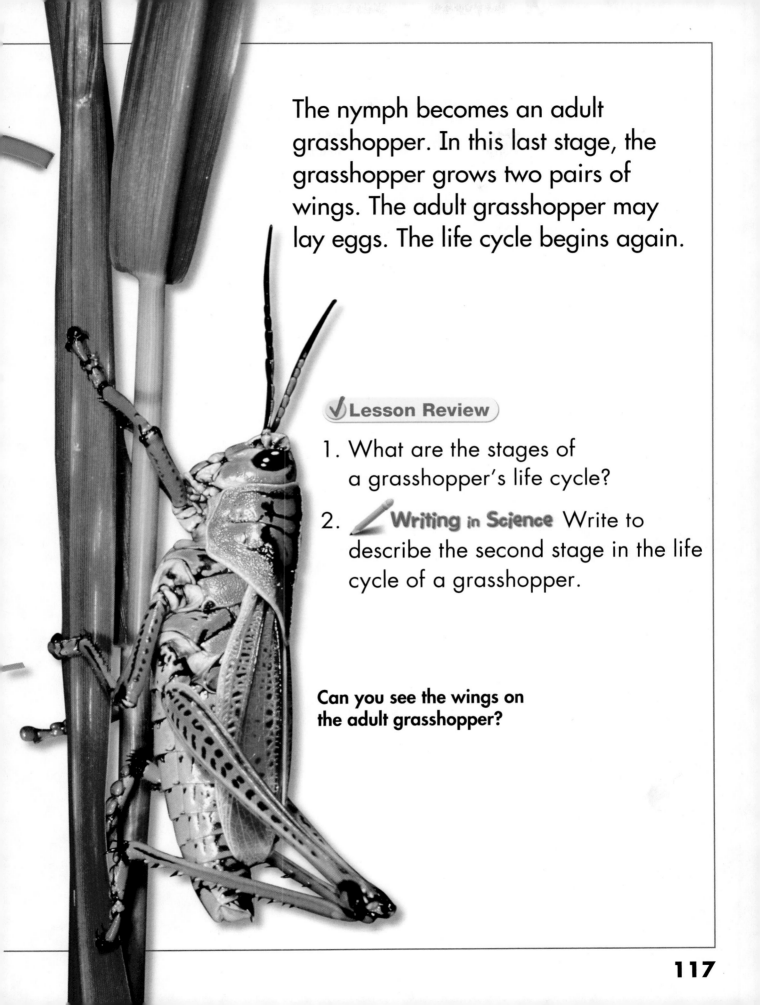

The nymph becomes an adult grasshopper. In this last stage, the grasshopper grows two pairs of wings. The adult grasshopper may lay eggs. The life cycle begins again.

✓ **Lesson Review**

1. What are the stages of a grasshopper's life cycle?

2. ✎ **Writing in Science** Write to describe the second stage in the life cycle of a grasshopper.

Can you see the wings on the adult grasshopper?

How Much Time?

These pictures show the life cycle of a butterfly. They show the amount of time between stages in the life cycle.

A butterfly life cycle

1. egg

2. caterpillar

4 days

12 days

3. pupa

14 days

4. butterfly

1. How many days does it take a butterfly egg to hatch into a caterpillar?

2. How many days does it take for a butterfly egg to become a butterfly? Write a number sentence.

3. If a caterpillar is 8 days old, how many more days will it take to become a pupa?

Lab zone Take-Home Activity

A caterpillar grows to be about 5 centimeters long. What other things might be 5 centimeters long? Measure to find out.

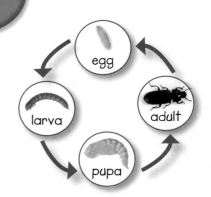

egg

larva

adult

pupa

Investigate What is the life cycle of a grain beetle?

Watch how mealworms grow. They change into grain beetles.

Materials

mealworms in habitat cup

magnifier

crayons and markers

What to Do

1 **Observe** the mealworms.

They are alive! Handle with care.

Process Skills

You can **observe** small things better using a magnifier. You **collect data** when you draw and describe what you observe.

2 **Collect Data** Draw the 2 stages you see.

larva

pupa

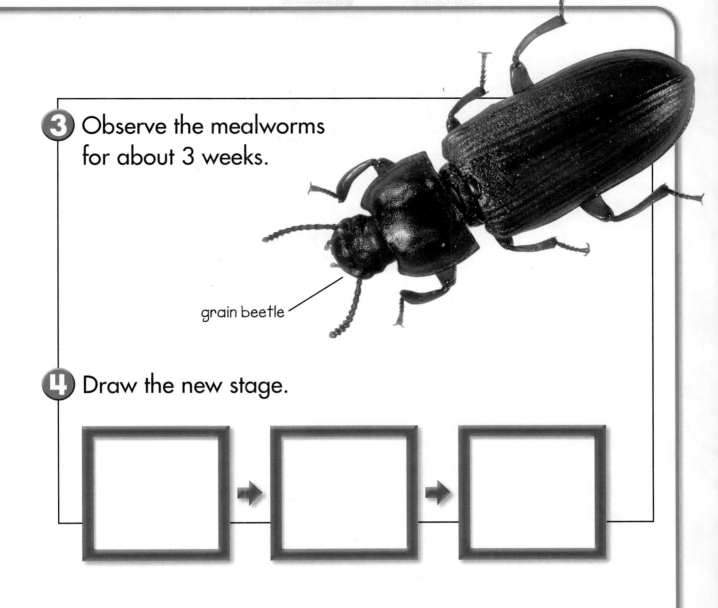

3 Observe the mealworms for about 3 weeks.

grain beetle

4 Draw the new stage.

☐ → ☐ → ☐

Explain Your Results

1. **Interpret Data** How did the mealworms change?
2. **Infer** What happens in the pupa stage?

Go Further

Can you make models of the stages in a mealworm's life cycle? Try it.

Focus on the BIG Idea

Animals grow and change during their life cycle. Different animals have different life cycles.

Lesson 1

What is a life cycle?

- A life cycle is the way a living thing grows and changes.
- Life cycles are different for different animals.

Lesson 2

What is the life cycle of a frog?

- The stages of the life cycle of a frog are egg, tadpole, young frog, and adult frog.

Lesson 3

What is the life cycle of a mouse?

- The life cycle of a mouse is the way a newborn mouse changes and grows into an adult mouse.

Lesson 4

What is the life cycle of a butterfly?

- The stages of the life cycle of a butterfly are egg, larva, pupa, and adult butterfly.

Lesson 5

What is the life cycle of a grasshopper?

- The stages of the life cycle of a grasshopper are egg, nymph, and adult grasshopper.

Cross-Curricular Links

English–Language Arts

Building Vocabulary

Look again at pages 100 and 101. Find the picture for the word *life cycle*. Write sentences about the life cycle of a frog. Tell about each stage of the life cycle. Read your sentences.

Mathematics

Finding the Number of Days

A young mouse goes outside the nest when it is about 2 weeks old. How many days are in 2 weeks? Write a number sentence.

Visual and Performing Arts

Drawing a Life Cycle

The steps in the life cycle of a butterfly are egg, larva, pupa, and adult. Draw pictures to show the life cycle of a butterfly. Color your pictures.

Challenge!
English–Language Arts

Writing About a Life Cycle

Find out about the life cycle of a sea turtle. Write a letter to your friend. Tell what you learned about the life cycle of a sea turtle. Remember to include the date, salutation, closing, and signature.

Vocabulary

Which picture goes with each word?

1. mammal (page 106)

2. amphibian (page 107)

3. insect (page 106)

4. tadpole (page 108)

5. larva (page 114)

6. pupa (page 114)

Think About It

7. Describe the life cycle of a frog. (pages 108–111)

8. How is a mammal different from an amphibian? (pages 106–107)

9. *Writing in Science* Tell how a mouse grows and changes. (pages 112–113)

10. *Process Skills* **Infer** Suppose you see an insect that looks like a tiny grasshopper. It does not have wings, but has a hard outside covering. What is it? (pages 116–117)

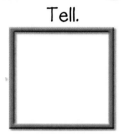

11. 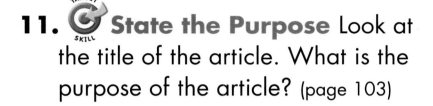 **State the Purpose** Look at the title of the article. What is the purpose of the article? (page 103)

Tell.

> **Life Cycle of a Salamander**
> There are three stages in the life cycle of a salamander. The stages are egg, larva, and adult.

California Standards Practice

Write the letter of the correct answer.

12. What is the second stage in the life cycle of a butterfly?

   A pupa

   B egg

   C butterfly

   D caterpillar

13. Look at the picture. What stage comes after the egg?

   A nymph

   B tadpole

   C pupa

   D larva

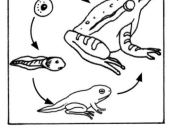

125

Animals at Kennedy Space Center

Read Together

Kennedy Space Center is on Merritt Island in Florida. Kennedy Space Center is part of a wildlife refuge. A wildlife refuge keeps animals safe.

More than 500 different types of animals live on and around Merritt Island. Some of the animals that live on Merritt Island cannot be found in many places in the country. The wildlife refuge protects the animals so that their life cycles can continue.

Bald Eagles

The nests of bald eagles on the wildlife refuge are safe. The eggs in the nest will hatch and grow into adults.

Sea Turtles

Sea turtles lay their eggs on land. Their eggs are safe on the refuge. The young sea turtles will soon live in the ocean.

Manatees

Manatees swim in the Banana River on the refuge. They are safe here.

Lab zone Take-Home Activity

Draw a picture of an animal that lives on Merritt Island. Tell your family about the animal.

SAVE the Sea Turtles

Meet Mario J. Mota

Read Together

Dr. Mota

Dr. Mario Mota is a marine biologist. He works at NASA. Dr. Mota studies turtle nests. He uses some of the tools used on the space shuttle to study the turtles.

Dr. Mota was born in Africa. He liked to fish when he was young. Dr. Mota always loved the ocean. He knew he wanted to work by the ocean.

Sea turtles lay their eggs on or near the same beach where they hatched. They lay more than 100 eggs in each nest!

Lab zone Take-Home Activity

Baby sea turtles hatch from eggs. Work with your family. Make a list of other animals that hatch from eggs.

CALIFORNIA
Standards
Focus Questions

- What do plants need to grow?
- How can the environment change the way plants grow?
- How do flowers, seeds, and fruits help plants grow?

Chapter 5

All About Plants

How do plants grow and change?

stem

pollen

germinate

Germinate means to begin to grow into a young plant.

DIGITAL g

seedling

seed coat

131

Explore How can light affect how a plant grows?

Materials

cup with seedling

water

prepared box with a lid

1 index card

tape

What to Do

1 Place your plant in the box. Put on the lid. Put the box in bright light.

2 When the plant reaches the first card, add the other card. Use tape.

Use tape to hold the other card here.

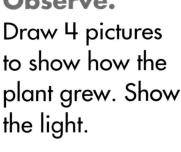

3 **Observe.** Draw 4 pictures to show how the plant grew. Show the light.

Process Skills

Writing or drawing your **observations** helps you **communicate.**

Explain Your Results

Communicate Write how light affected your plant.

How to Read Science

TARGET SKILL

Main Idea and Details

A main idea is the most important idea about what you have read. Details tell more about the main idea.

Science Article

How Temperature Can Change a Plant

Temperature can change how a plant grows. It is hard for some plants to stay healthy when it is too hot or too cold. Cold temperatures can cause a plant to freeze. A frozen plant will die. Hot temperatures can also cause some plants to die.

Apply It!

Communicate

Read the article. What is the main idea? What are three details about the main idea?

Main Idea

Detail	Detail	Detail

Plants

Sung to the tune of "Where, Oh, Where Has My Little Dog Gone?"
Lyrics by Gerri Brioso & Richard Freitas/The Dovetail Group, Inc.

All plants have roots that grow in soil,
And hold the plant in place.
The roots take in water and nutrients,
And carry them up to the stem.

Lesson 1

What do plants need to grow?

Plants need water, air, and sunlight to grow. Plants need nutrients from the soil too. Nutrients help plants grow.

Plant Parts

Plants have four main parts. The four main parts are the roots, stem, leaves, and flowers.

Gravity causes roots to grow down into the soil. Roots hold the plant in place. Roots take water and nutrients from the soil. Roots carry water and nutrients to the stem.

The **stem** carries water and nutrients to the leaves. The stem holds up the plant.

Roots

Green leaves use air, water, and energy from light to make food for the plant.

Flowers make seeds. Seeds can grow into new plants.

Flower

Stem

Leaves

Stems and leaves grow toward light.

Lesson Review

TARGET SKILL

1. What do plants need to grow?

2. **Main Idea and Details** What is the main idea of these two pages? What are details that support the main idea?

How can the environment change the way plants grow?

Changes in the environment can change the way a plant grows. Plants need just the right amount of sunlight and water to grow and stay healthy. Plants that do not get enough of what they need may not grow.

Some plants may not live without water.

The green leaves show that this plant has had enough sunlight.

Changes in temperature can change the way a plant grows. If it is too hot or too cold, some plants may not stay healthy.

Leaves can turn yellow when plants do not get enough sunlight.

Cold temperatures may harm a plant.

Look for Active Art animations at www.pearsonsuccessnet.com

1. ✓**Checkpoint** What happens when plants don't get enough sunlight or water?

2. How can changes in temperature change the way plants grow?

Other Changes in Plants

Other things can change the way plants grow. The tree in the picture is growing in a very windy place. The wind made the tree bend. This type of tree can grow straight in places that are not windy.

Vines are plants with long, thin stems. Vines can grow along the ground. Vines can grow in different ways when they touch objects. They can grow up a wall. You might even see vines growing on another plant.

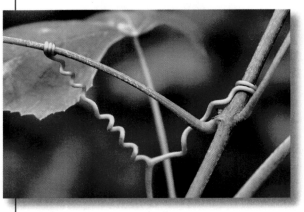

This grapevine has attached itself to another plant.

You know that plants need nutrients to grow. Nutrients come from soil. Some kinds of soil do not have enough nutrients. Plants may not grow well in soil that does not have enough nutrients.

This corn plant gets the nutrients it needs to grow from the soil.

Lesson Review

1. What can happen when a vine touches another object?

2. Writing in Science Write about some things that can change the way a plant grows.

How do flowers, seeds, and fruits help plants grow?

Petal

Look at the flower on this page. The outside part of the flower is called a petal. Petals are often colored. A powder called **pollen** is found inside the flower. Pollen is needed to make seeds grow.

Fruit is formed around the seeds as they grow. The fruit protects the seeds. The seeds will make new plants. You can see the seeds inside apples, oranges, and ears of corn.

Pollen

Seed coat

Each seed contains a tiny new plant. A seed has a hard outer covering called a seed coat. The **seed coat** protects the new plant. Food is stored around the new plant. The plant uses the stored food as it grows.

A magnifying glass can help you take a closer look inside the flower.

1. ✓ Checkpoint What is a seed coat?

2. ✎ Writing in Science Tell how flowers and fruits help plants grow.

The Life Cycle of a Peach Tree

Many kinds of plants grow from seeds. A peach tree is a plant that grows from a seed.

First, a peach seed is planted. A seed that gets enough water and air may **germinate,** or begin to grow. Roots grow down into the ground. The stem of a young plant begins to grow up from the ground. The young plant is called a **seedling.**

The seedling will grow and change. It will become an adult peach tree. New trees may grow from the fruit of the adult tree.

Seed

A peach tree begins as a seed. The peach seed germinates.

A young peach tree, or seedling, grows from the seed.

Fruit forms with seeds inside. The seeds may grow into a new peach tree. The life cycle begins again.

The seedling grows into an adult peach tree. Flowers will begin to grow on the peach tree.

✓ **Lesson Review**

1. What is the first stage in the life cycle of a peach tree?

TARGET SKILL

2. **Main Idea and Details** What is the main idea of this lesson? What are the details?

Compare Growing Times

Some vegetables take longer than others to grow. If you plant green bean seeds, how soon can you eat the beans that will grow?

Green bean

Cucumber

Sweet corn

Carrot

Look at the table. The table tells you which seeds were planted. The table also tells you how many days it will be until each vegetable is ready to eat.

Days from Planting to Eating

Type of Plant	Number of Days
green bean	58 Days
cucumber	55 Days
sweet corn	75 Days
carrot	70 Days

1 Which plants take the most number of days to grow?

2 Suppose you plant carrot seeds. How many days will there be until you can eat carrots?

3 How many more days does it take sweet corn to grow than cucumbers? Write a number sentence.

Lab zone Take-Home Activity

Find out how long it takes different kinds of flower seeds to grow and bloom. Make a table to show what you find.

Guided Inquiry

Investigate How can gravity affect the growth of roots?

Materials

3 paper towels

graduated cylinder

water and cup

4 pinto bean seeds

masking tape

magnifier

What to Do

1 Fold a paper towel 2 times. Put it in the cup, around the sides.

2 Wad up 2 paper towels, stuff them in the center of the cup. Pour 50 mL of water on the towels to moisten them.

3 Poke in the 4 seeds.

Label the cup A, B, C, and D. The seeds MUST be in these 4 positions in the cup.

front of cup   back of cup

DIGITAL Lab zone

4 Put the cup in a warm place. **Observe** the seeds daily for a week. Use a magnifier. Keep towels moist. Water if needed.

5 Draw how the roots grew.

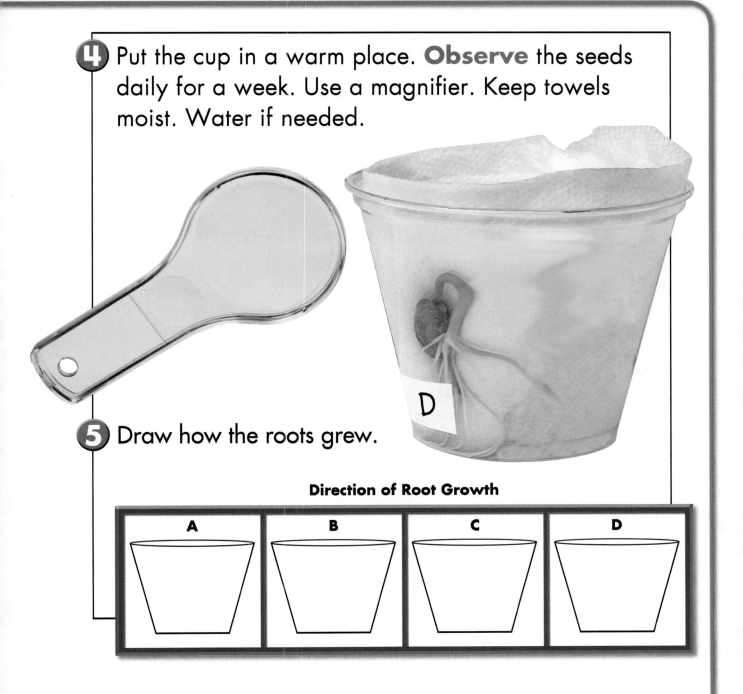

Direction of Root Growth

A	B	C	D

Explain Your Results

1. **Interpret Data** What direction did the 4 roots grow?
2. Draw a conclusion about how gravity affects the growth of roots.

Go Further

Does temperature affect seed growth? Plant seeds in warm and cold places. Measure and record the temperatures. Tell what you learn.

Focus on the BIG Idea

Plants grow and change when they get the water, air, sunlight, and nutrients they need. Flowers, seeds, and fruit help new plants grow.

Lesson 1

What do plants need to grow?

- Plants need water, air, sunlight, and nutrients to grow.
- The parts of a plant help the plant get what it needs.

Lesson 2

How can the environment change the way plants grow?

- Plants that do not get the right amount of sunlight or water may not grow.
- If it is too hot or too cold, some plants may not stay healthy.
- The way plants grow can change when they touch other objects.
- Wind can change the way a plant grows.

Lesson 3

How do flowers, seeds, and fruits help plants grow?

- Seeds grow inside of flowers.
- Fruit grows around seeds.
- New plants grow from seeds.

Cross-Curricular Links

English–Language Arts

Building Vocabulary

Look again at pages 130 and 131. Write a story about a seed that is planted. Tell what will happen when the seed is watered. Use the word *germinate* in your story.

Mathematics

The Height of Corn

Maria planted corn in her garden. The corn was 60 cm tall after two months. It grew 80 cm in the next two months. How tall was the corn after four months?

Health

Healthy Food Choices

Work with a partner. Talk about healthy food choices. What types of healthy food can be grown in a garden or on a farm?

Challenge!

History–Social Science

Types of Plants

You have learned about the ways different types of plants grow and change. Choose a California county other than yours. Find out about what types of plants grow well in that county. Write sentences to tell what you learned.

Vocabulary

Which picture goes with each word?

1. stem (page 136)

2. pollen (page 142)

3. seed coat (page 143)

4. seedling (page 144)

Think About It

5. Tell what happens when a seed germinates. (page 144)

6. ✎ **Writing in Science** Explain how sunlight might change the way a plant grows. (pages 137–139)

7. **Process Skills** **Communicate** Tell which of these are parts of a plant: roots, stem, germinate, flower, or nutrients. (pages 136–137)

8. **TARGET SKILL** **Main Idea and Details** What is the main idea of this chapter? What are three important details? (pages 133, 135–145)

Main Idea		
Detail	Detail	Detail

California Standards Practice

Write the letter of the correct answer.

9. What is the first stage in the life cycle of a peach tree?

   A flowers

   B seedling

   C fruit

   D seed

10. Look at the picture. What are the four main parts of a plant?

   A roots, stem, leaves, petals

   B roots, stem, leaves, flower

   C roots, pollen, leaves, petals

   D roots, pollen, leaves, flower

Mary Agnes Chase

Read Together

Mary Agnes Chase was born in 1869. She liked to collect plants when she was young. Mary Agnes drew pictures of the plants she collected.

When she was older, Mary Agnes Chase became a plant scientist. She traveled all over the world studying plants and drawing pictures of them.

Mary Agnes Chase wrote books to help other people learn about plants. Her drawings were included in the books she wrote.

Mary Agnes Chase enjoyed learning about and drawing grasses.

Lab zone Take-Home Activity

Find a grass plant or other plant growing outside. Draw a picture of it. Talk to your family about your drawing.

Unit B Summary

Chapter 3

Why do plants and animals look the way they do?
- Young plants and animals inherit some things from their parents.
- Animals look like their parents and each other, but may be different colors and different sizes.

Chapter 4

How do animals grow and change?
- Different animals grow and change in different ways.
- A life cycle is the way a living thing grows and changes.

Chapter 5

How do plants grow and change?
- Plants need water, air, sunlight, and nutrients to grow.
- Changes in the environment can change the way plants grow.
- Plants have life cycles.

Experiment How can soil affect the growth of plants?

Materials

3 small paper cups with holes in the bottom

30 radish seeds

water

spoon

graduated cylinder

thermometer (optional)

clay soil

sandy soil

loam soil

Ask a question.
How does the kind of soil affect how many radish seeds will grow?

Make a hypothesis.
Suppose you planted radish seeds in clay soil, sandy soil, and loam soil. In which kind of soil will the most plants grow?

Plan a fair test.
Make sure the cups get the same amount of light. Keep the cups at the same temperature. Use the same amount of soil. Use the same amount of water.

Do your test.

1 Put one kind of soil in each cup.

2 Sprinkle 10 radish seeds in each cup.

Spread a thin layer of soil over the seeds in each cup.

sandy soil

clay soil

loam soil

Label the cups.

3 Add 15 mL of water to each cup. Use a graduated cylinder.

4 Put the cups in a bright place. **Observe** and water for 3 weeks. How many plants are growing?

Number of Plants Growing after 3 Weeks

Number of Plants Growing

10
9
8
7
6
5
4
3
2
1
0

clay soil   sandy soil   loam soil

Types of Soil

Collect and record data.
Make a bar graph.

Tell your conclusion.
In which type of soil did the most radish plants grow?

Go Further
How well would other seeds grow in the soils you used? Find out the answer to this question or a question of your own.

Draw a Picture of the Life Cycle of a Peach Tree

- Draw a picture of a peach tree's life cycle.

- Label each stage in your picture.

- Tell your class about how a seed grows and changes.

Write a Folktale

A folktale is a story that has been handed down from older people to younger people for many years. Think of a fruit you like that grows on trees. Then write a folktale about a family that lived long ago and planted fruit trees of that kind.

Read More About Life Sciences

Look for other books about Life Sciences in your library-media center.

One book you may want to read is:

The Tiny Seed
by Eric Carle

This book follows a plant through its life cycle as a tiny seed, a growing plant, and a big, beautiful flower.

Science Fair Projects

Using Scientific Methods
1. Ask a question.
2. Make a hypothesis.
3. Plan a fair test.
4. Do your test.
5. Collect and record data.
6. Tell your conclusion.
7. Go further.

Idea 1
Temperature and Seeds

Plan a project. Find out if seeds will grow faster in a warm place or in a cold place.

Idea 2
Sunlight and Plants

Plan an experiment. Find out how much sunlight is best for one kind of plant.

Unit B California Standards Practice

Write the letter of the correct answer.

1. What do oak trees drop that grow into new oak trees?

 A roots

 B stems

 C acorns

 D leaves

2. Look at the picture. What do young rabbits inherit from their parents?

 A short ears and a long tail

 B fuzzy down feathers and beaks

 C small eyes and short ears

 D long ears, large eyes, and a short tail

3. **What are offspring?**

A young plants and animals

B parents of young plants and animals

C animals that have hair or fur on their bodies

D everything around a living thing

4. **What is a young grasshopper called?**

A larva

B tadpole

C nymph

D pupa

5. **What does a young mouse look like when it is born?**

    A It looks exactly like its parents.

    B It has a lot of hair.

    C Its eyes are open and it has fuzzy down feathers.

    D It does not have hair and its eyes are closed.

6. **Which of the following can change the way a plant grows?**

    A too much pollen

    B the amount of light the plant gets

    C the way the seed germinates

    D not enough wind

7. What is found inside fruit?

    A pollen that bees will carry to a flower
    B flowers that will lose their petals
    C seeds that may grow into new plants
    D roots that will make food for new plants

8. What happens when some plants do not get enough water?

    A They might die.
    B They might turn green.
    C They might grow more flowers.
    D They might get larger.

Earth Sciences

The Page Museum
Rancho La Brea Tar Pits

Los Angeles, California

Come and take a look at life long ago! The La Brea Tar Pits is one of the world's most famous fossil sites. Here, you can see life-size models of many animals from long ago.

You can visit the Page Museum and learn how a tar pit formed. You will also learn how fossils formed.

Los Angeles

Find out more.

- Research to find out more about the La Brea Tar Pits and the Page Museum.

- Make a book of pictures that shows what you can see and do at the La Brea Tar Pits.

The Page Museum and the La Brea Tar Pits

- What are rocks and minerals?
- What is weathering?
- What is soil?
- What are natural resources?

Chapter 6

Rocks and Soil

What are some of Earth's natural resources?

rock

weathering

Chapter 6 Vocabulary

minerals

luster

soil

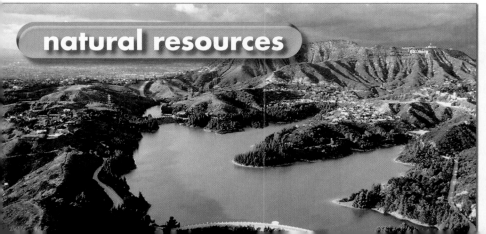

natural resources

fuel

Explore How can you compare properties of Earth materials?

Materials

earth materials

magnifier

balance and
gram cubes

What to Do

1 Sort the samples by luster.
Luster is how shiny they are.

2 Sort the samples by weight.
Use grams.

Explain Your Results
Share your **observations.**
What are some other ways
you can sort your samples?

How to Read Science

TARGET SKILL

Draw Conclusions

You can use what you observe or read to help you **draw a conclusion.**

Science Story

How Soil Helps Plants Grow

Most plants grow in soil. Some soils make plants grow better. Plants need water to grow. Soil holds the water that plants need. Sandy soil does not hold water well.

Apply It!

What might you **observe** if you grew a plant in sandy soil?

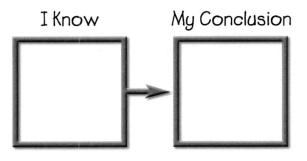

I Know   My Conclusion

 DIGITAL

You Are There

Rocks Rock!

Sung to the tune of "A Tisket A Tasket"
Lyrics by Gerri Brioso & Richard Freitas/The Dovetail Group, Inc.

A rock here, A rock there.

You can find rocks everywhere!

In my yard I found a few,

And then found more inside my shoe!

DIGITAL

What are rocks and minerals?

Rocks are everywhere! You might find rocks in your backyard, at the beach, or in a forest. A **rock** is the hard, solid part of the Earth that is not soil or metal.

Rocks can be different colors. Some rocks are smooth. Other rocks are very rough.

Rocks can be different sizes too. You can hold some rocks in your hand. They are very light. Other rocks are as big as a tree. They are very heavy.

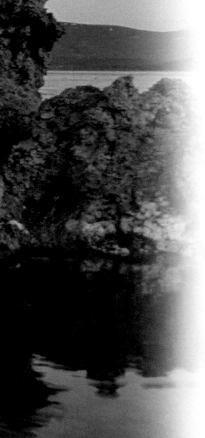

Look at these rocks. What are some ways they are different?

Minerals

Rocks are made up of minerals. **Minerals** are nonliving materials that come from Earth. Some minerals are gold, silver, and iron. Many things are made from minerals. Some rings are made from gold. Some coins have silver in them. Some nails are made from iron.

Most rocks are made up of more than one mineral. Look at the big piece of granite. It is made up of three minerals. The minerals are quartz, feldspar, and mica. You can see each kind of mineral in the piece of granite.

Silver is a mineral. Silver is used to make coins and jewelry.

Granite is a pink or gray rock.

Quartz

Feldspar

Mica

1. ✓ Checkpoint What are rocks made of?

2. What are some kinds of minerals?

DIGITAL

NSTA
SciLinks
keyword: minerals
code: gr2p174

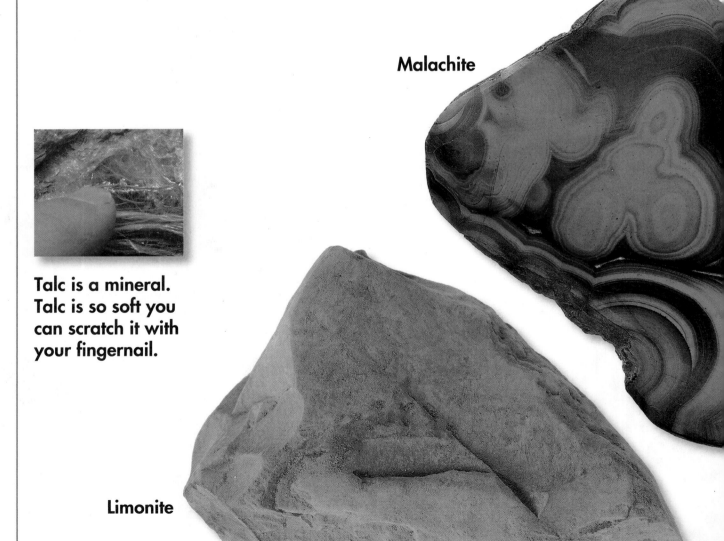

Properties of Minerals

Minerals have different properties. A property is something about an object that you can observe. Minerals can be hard or soft. This property is called hardness.

Another property of minerals is color. Look at the three minerals below. Limonite is yellow. Malachite is green. Azurite is blue.

A diamond is the hardest mineral found on Earth. A diamond can scratch glass.

Talc is a mineral. Talc is so soft you can scratch it with your fingernail.

Malachite

Limonite

Minerals can be shiny or dull. This property is called **luster.** Limonite has a dull luster. Azurite has a shiny luster.

✓ Lesson Review

1. What are three properties of minerals?

2. **Draw Conclusions** What would happen if you rubbed a diamond across a piece of glass?

Azurite

What is weathering?

Weathering changes a rock's size, shape, and color. **Weathering** is the breaking apart and changing of rocks.

Look at the picture at the bottom of the page. Weathering can turn large boulders into smaller rocks. Weathering can turn these smaller rocks into grains of sand.

Weathering can change large rocks into small grains of sand!

Large rocks

Weathering can be caused by water and by changes in temperature. Water can be found in the cracks of a big rock. The rock breaks apart when the water freezes and turns to ice.

Weathering caused by ice

Weathering can be caused by plant growth. The roots of a plant can grow in the cracks of a rock. As the roots grow, they can break apart the rock.

Weathering caused by roots

1. ✓Checkpoint What is weathering?

2. What can cause weathering?

Small rocks   Gravel   Sand

Other Causes of Weathering

Look at the picture of a cave below. Water in the ground dissolved lots of rock. The water carried the dissolved rock away. Dripping water caused the shapes hanging from the roof of the cave. Dripping water caused the shapes on the floor of the cave too. Columns form when the two shapes join.

DIGITAL
Look for Active Art animations at www.pearsonsuccessnet.com

Have you ever been inside a cave?

Iron can be found in some rocks. When these rocks get wet, the iron mixes with air. Rust is formed. The rocks become a reddish brown color. The rocks become weaker and may break apart.

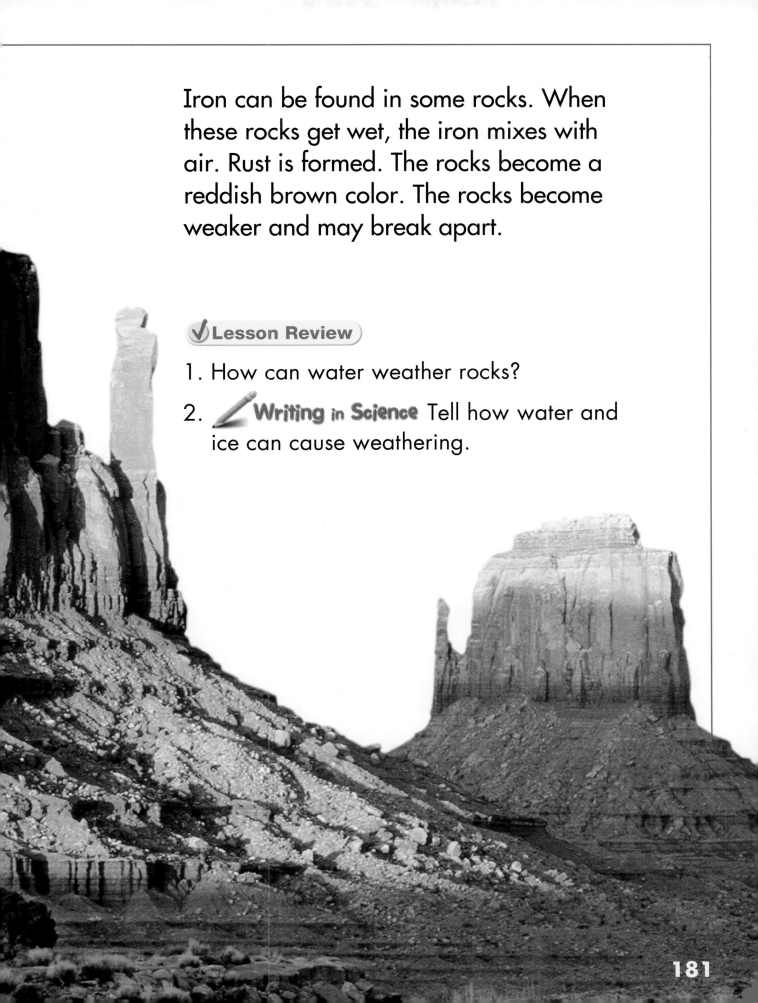

✔ Lesson Review

1. How can water weather rocks?

2. ✎ **Writing in Science** Tell how water and ice can cause weathering.

What is soil?

Soil is the top layer of Earth. Plants grow in soil. Look at the picture of soil. You can see many things that make up the soil.

Weathered rock and other kinds of material can be found in soil. Leaves, twigs, and other living things that have died are found in soil.

Animals can change the soil by digging in it. Digging loosens and mixes the soil.

Gophers loosen and mix soil. This helps plants grow.

1. ✓Checkpoint What is soil?

2. What things can you find in soil?

Worms loosen and mix the soil.

Kinds of Soil

Different kinds of plants grow best in different kinds of soil. Sandy soil is not good for most plants. Sandy soil does not hold water well. It is found in deserts and near oceans and lakes.

Clay soil holds water, but some plants do not grow well in it. The red color of some clay comes from iron in the soil.

Sandy soil feels dry and rough.

Clay soil feels smooth.
It feels soft and sticky too.

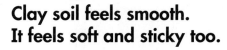

Loam is a dark color. Loam is clay and sand mixed with pieces of plants and animals that have died.

Loam is the best soil for growing most kinds of plants. Loam holds water well. Plants are able to get the water they need to grow.

✓ Lesson Review

1. What are three kinds of soil?

2. **Draw Conclusions** What kind of soil would you use to grow most plants? Why?

What are natural resources?

Resources are things that people can use. Soil, water, rocks, and plants are natural resources. **Natural resources** are useful materials that come from Earth.

Cotton is a natural resource.
Cotton comes from a plant.
We use cotton to make clothes.

Trees are a natural resource.
We use wood from trees to
build houses and furniture.

Natural resources meet many of our needs. We use natural resources for food, clothing, shelter, and fuel. Rocks can be used for building things. Soil is used to grow plants for food. Plants can also be used for fuel and to build things.

1. ✓Checkpoint What is a natural resource?

2. What are some ways we use plants as natural resources?

All plants are natural resources. Farmers grow many kinds of plants for food.

Water is a natural resource. Plants need water to grow. We need to drink water to stay healthy.

Other Natural Resources

You know that rocks are a natural resource. Rocks can be used to build things. Rocks can be mixed with sand, cement, and water. This mixture is called concrete. Concrete is used to build roads, sidewalks, and steps.

These steps are made of concrete.

Wood is used for fuel in a fireplace. A fireplace can help heat our homes.

Wood, oil, and gas are natural resources. They are used for fuel. **Fuel** is anything that is burned to make heat or power. Oil and gas come from plants and animals that lived long ago.

Gasoline is a fuel. A car's engine burns gas so that it has the energy to move.

✓ **Lesson Review**

1. What is fuel?

2. ✎ **Writing in Science** Tell about ways people use natural resources every day.

Sorting Minerals

Anna has a rock collection. She has 4 different colors of rocks. Anna sorted the rocks by color. The table shows how many rocks she has of each color.

Color	Number of Rocks
Black	12
Gray	37
White	12
Pink	24

Use the table. Write the number of rocks Anna has of each color. Replace the circle with <, =, or >.

1 pink ◯ gray

2 black ◯ white

3 pink ◯ white

4 Write the numbers from the table in order from least to greatest. Use the number 12 only once.

Lab zone Take-Home Activity

Take a walk outdoors. Look at the different kinds of rocks. Sort them based on two or more differences. Use color, texture, and shape.

Investigate How can you compare and sort minerals and rocks?

Materials

magnifier

simple microscope

minerals and rocks

Process Skills

Magnifiers and microscopes can help you to **observe** and draw descriptions of small things.

What to Do

1 **Observe** the quartz (A).
Use a magnifier.
Use a simple microscope.

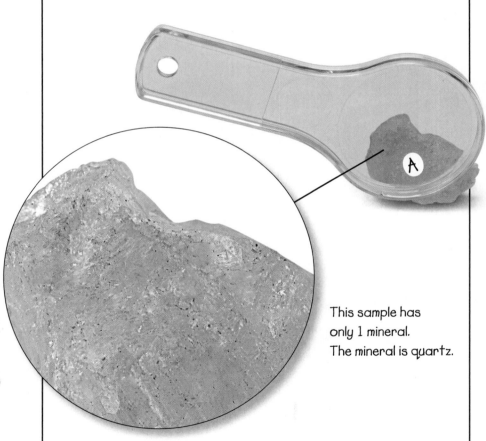

This sample has only 1 mineral. The mineral is quartz.

2 Observe the feldspar (B) and mica (C). Each has only 1 mineral.

3 Observe the granite (D). Look for little grains. Some are white. Others are pink or gray. Draw the granite. Show the grains.

Granite has 3 minerals.

4 Observe the gabbro (E) and diorite (F). Look for grains. Draw.

How many minerals are in hornblende (G)?

5 **Classify** Sort the samples based on how many minerals are in each sample.

Group	Samples in Group
Has only 1 mineral	
Has more than 1 mineral	

The samples are about the same size. Are some heavier? Find out.

Explain Your Results
Tell how you sorted your samples using what you **observed.**

Go Further
Sort your samples based on two or more differences. Use size, shape, color, weight, hardness, or luster.

Focus on the BIG Idea

Rocks and minerals are some of Earth's natural resources. Plants, soil, and water are also natural resources.

Lesson 1

What are rocks and minerals?

- A rock is a hard, solid part of the Earth that is not soil or metal.
- Rocks are made of minerals.
- Color, luster, and hardness are properties of minerals.

Lesson 2

What is weathering?

- Weathering is the breaking apart and changing of rocks.
- Weathering turns rocks into sand.
- Weathering can be caused by water, changes in temperature, or by plant roots.

Lesson 3

What is soil?

- Soil is the top layer of Earth.
- Some kinds of soil hold water better than others.

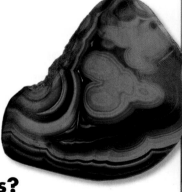

Lesson 4

What are natural resources?

- Natural resources are useful materials that come from Earth.
- Natural resources can be used for food, clothing, shelter, and fuel.

Cross-Curricular Links

English–Language Arts

Building Vocabulary

Look again at pages 168–169. Find the picture for the words *minerals* and *luster*. Write sentences about two kinds of minerals and tell about their luster. Read your sentences.

Mathematics

Estimating Size

Think about a rock you can hold in your hand. Will the length of the rock be closer to 10 centimeters, 30 centimeters, or 1 meter?

Visual and Performing Arts

Weathered Rocks

Draw a picture. Show one way weathering can change a rock. Color your picture.

Challenge!

English–Language Arts

Natural Resources

You know that trees are a natural resource used to build houses. Find out how trees are cut down to make wood used for building houses. Write a paragraph to tell what you have learned. Be sure to include each step.

Vocabulary

Which picture goes with each word?

1. rock (page 173)

2. minerals (page 174)

3. luster (page 177)

4. weathering (page 178)

5. soil (page 182)

6. fuel (page 189)

A

B

C

D

E

F

Think About It

7. Why are natural resources important? (pages 186–189)

8. Why is soil important? (pages 182–185)

9. **Writing in Science** Write two sentences. Tell about the properties of minerals. (pages 176–177)

10. **Process Skills** **Predict** Suppose you look inside a cave where water is dripping. What might you see? (page 180)

11. **Draw Conclusions**
Suppose you see water in the
cracks of a big rock. What do
you think will happen?
(pages 178–179)

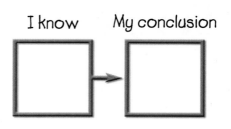

I know   My conclusion

California Standards Practice

Write the letter of the correct answer.

12. Which best describes sandy soil?

   A feels smooth and sticky

   B feels dry and rough

   C made of living things

   D has a shiny luster

13. Look at the picture. What does it show?

   A luster

   B sand

   C loam

   D weathering

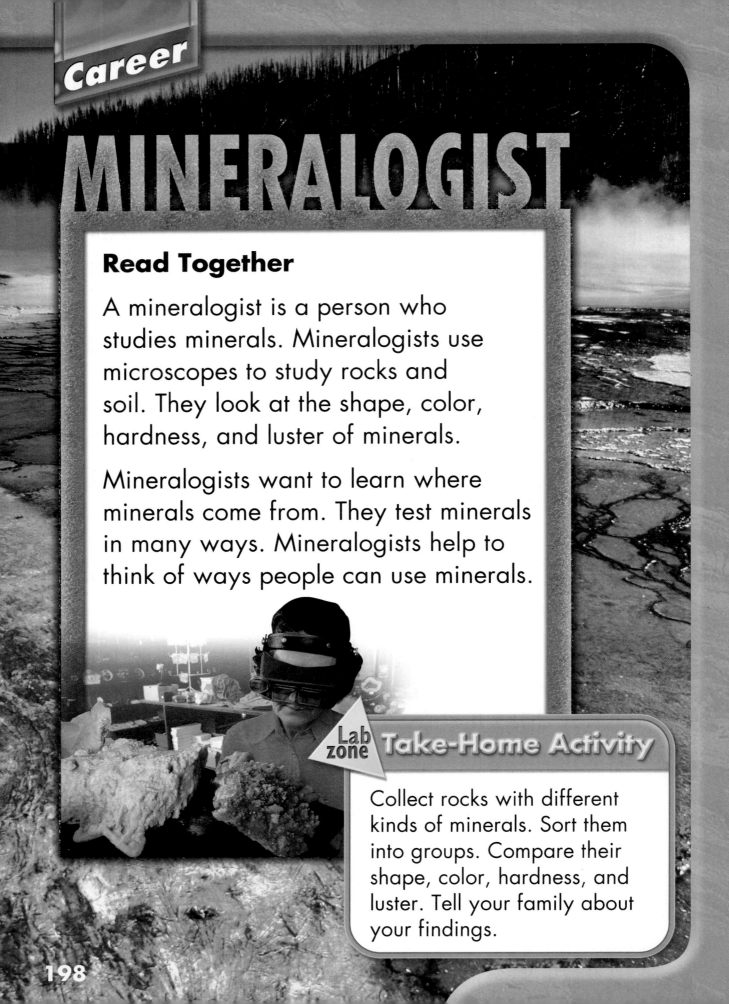

MINERALOGIST

Read Together

A mineralogist is a person who studies minerals. Mineralogists use microscopes to study rocks and soil. They look at the shape, color, hardness, and luster of minerals.

Mineralogists want to learn where minerals come from. They test minerals in many ways. Mineralogists help to think of ways people can use minerals.

Lab zone Take-Home Activity

Collect rocks with different kinds of minerals. Sort them into groups. Compare their shape, color, hardness, and luster. Tell your family about your findings.

Chapter 7

Fossils and Dinosaurs

CALIFORNIA
Standards Focus Questions

- What is a fossil?
- How do we learn about life long ago?
- What were dinosaurs like?
- How are plants and animals of long ago like those today?

How can people learn about Earth long ago?

dinosaur

fossil

DIGITAL

skeleton

Directed Inquiry

Explore How can you study fossils?

Materials

Dinosaur Bone Cutouts

scissors

masking tape

What to Do

1 Cut out the bones.

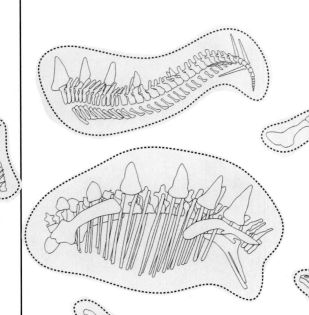

2 Fit the dinosaur's bones together.

Explain Your Results

Describe how you put the **model** together. Write what you did first, next, and last.

How to Read Science

TARGET
SKILL

Use Graphic Organizers

You can organize information easily when you **use graphic organizers**. Graphic organizers can help you see how ideas are related to each other.

Science Story

Ichthyosaurs

An ichthyosaur was a reptile that lived long ago. It was part of the lizard family, but looked like a dolphin! It used its tail to move like a fish. An ichthyosaur ate fish.

Apply It!

Make and Use Models

Read the story above again. Use the graphic organizer to tell what you learned about ichthyosaurs.

Ichthyosaurs

You Are There

Go Find a Fossil

Sung to the tune of "Take Me Out to the Ballgame"
Lyrics by Gerri Brioso & Richard Freitas/The Dovetail Group, Inc.

Take a shovel, go digging.
In the dirt you may find,
Rocks that have shapes printed right in them.
Shapes of a leaf or an animal!

If you find one, you have a fossil,
A special clue to the past.
See what plants and animals looked like
A long time ago!

What is a fossil?

Have you ever seen a fossil? A **fossil** is a print or part of a plant or animal that lived long ago. Some fossils are very old bones. Other fossils are shapes that have been left in rocks.

Some scientists study fossils. They want to learn what plants and animals looked like long ago.

DIGITAL

NSTA
SciLinks

keyword:
fossil
code:
gr2p205

205

What Fossils Show

Fossils show the size and shape of plants and animals that lived long ago. Some fossils are of plants and animals that no longer live on Earth.

These fossils are of plants that lived long ago.

This fossil shows the shape of a lizard that lived long ago.

A Fossil Is Formed

A lizard dies.

The lizard is covered in sand and mud.

The sand and mud become rock.

✔ **Lesson Review**

1. What are fossils?

2. **Use Graphic Organizers** Write what you learned about fossils. Use a graphic organizer to help you.

TARGET SKILL

How do we learn about life long ago?

Scientists help us learn about life on Earth long ago. Fossils show clues about the past.

The scientist in the first picture below has found a fossil. He is using a brush to uncover the fossil.

The scientist in the second picture below is trying to build a skeleton from fossils of bones. A **skeleton** is all the bones of a body.

It can take a long time to uncover a fossil.

This scientist must be very careful not to break the bones!

1. 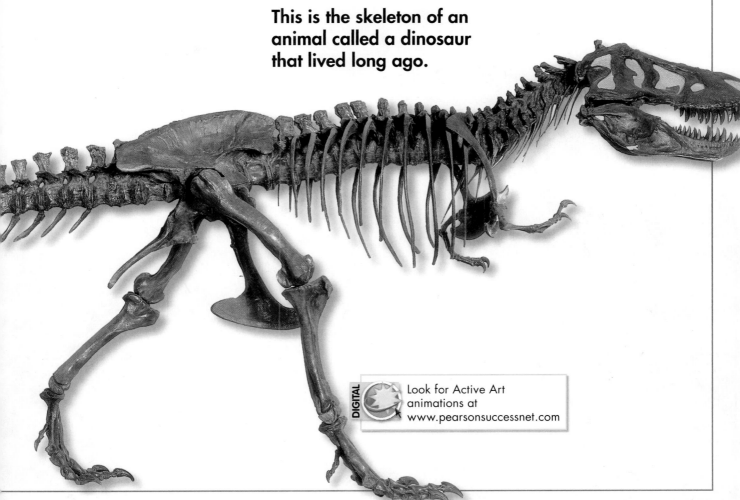 ✔ **Checkpoint** Why do scientists study fossils?

2. ✎ **Writing in Science** Tell what scientists do when they find a fossil.

This is the skeleton of an animal called a dinosaur that lived long ago.

DIGITAL
Look for Active Art animations at www.pearsonsuccessnet.com

Dinosaurs on Earth

Dinosaurs were animals that lived on Earth long ago. Scientists study fossils of dinosaur bones. They want to learn what dinosaurs looked like and how they lived.

Fossils can also show us how Earth has changed over time. Look at the picture. It shows what Earth might have looked like when dinosaurs lived on it.

1.  ✓Checkpoint What were dinosaurs?

2. What can fossils tell us about Earth?

New Discoveries

Scientists look for fossils all over the world. Some fossils show us new things about dinosaurs.

The skeleton of a tyrannosauroid was found in China. This dinosaur was about 2 meters long. It had feathers, but it could not fly. The feathers might have kept it warm. This dinosaur ate meat.

Skull of the tyrannosauroid

A drawing of a dinosaur called a tyrannosauroid

Scientists from China worked to rebuild the tyrannosauroid skeleton. The picture shows what this dinosaur might have looked like when it was alive.

✓ Lesson Review

1. Where did the tyrannosauroid live?

2. What did the tyrannosauroid eat?

Lesson 3

What were dinosaurs like?

Scientists learn many things by studying dinosaur fossils. Dinosaur fossils show that some dinosaurs were very big. Other dinosaurs were small.

A *Compsognathus* was about as long as a large chicken.

Compsognathus

Many kinds of dinosaurs lived on Earth long ago. There are no dinosaurs today.

1.  ✓Checkpoint How long was a *Compsognathus*?

2. Write in your science notebook. Tell about a dinosaur that once lived on Earth.

A *Gallimimus* was about as long as an elephant.

Gallimimus

Dinosaur Food

Scientists want to learn about the kinds of food dinosaurs ate. Some dinosaurs had long, sharp teeth. They ate meat. Some dinosaurs had short, flat teeth. They ate plants.

What big teeth! This is the skull of a *Tyrannosaurus rex*. It used its very sharp teeth to eat meat.

A *Tyrannosaurus rex* was one of the largest dinosaurs that ate meat.

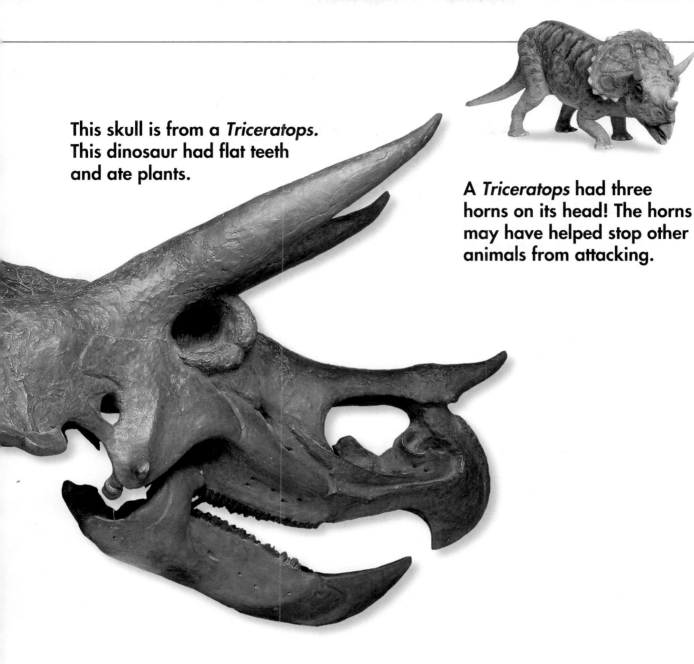

This skull is from a *Triceratops*. This dinosaur had flat teeth and ate plants.

A *Triceratops* had three horns on its head! The horns may have helped stop other animals from attacking.

√ Lesson Review

1. Why do scientists study fossils of dinosaur teeth?

2. **Use Graphic Organizers** Write what scientists learn about when they study fossils of dinosaur teeth. Use a graphic organizer to help you.

How are plants and animals of long ago like those today?

Scientists learn about animals by studying their footprints. Look at the *Iguanodon* footprint. Scientists believe that this dinosaur walked on its toes.

Look at the grizzly bear footprint. Bears have long claws and their toes are close together. Bears walk with their feet and toes flat on the ground.

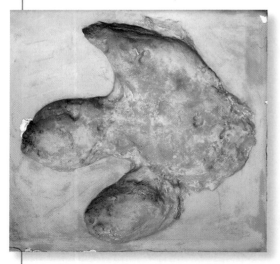

This is a footprint of an *Iguanodon*. Scientists learned about the size of an *Iguanodon* by studying its footprint.

This is a footprint of a grizzly bear today.

Some birds that lived long ago had feathers and beaks like birds today. Some had sharp teeth and long, bony tails. Most birds today do not have teeth or bony tails.

The *Archaeopteryx* was a bird that lived long ago. Can you see the wings and the beak in this fossil?

The Canada goose is a large bird that lives on Earth today.

1. ✓Checkpoint Why do scientists study dinosaur footprints?

2. ✏ Writing in Science How are birds from long ago like birds today? How are they different?

Plants Long Ago and Today

Plant fossils show the size and shape of plants that lived long ago. Scientists want to learn how plants that lived long ago were like plants today.

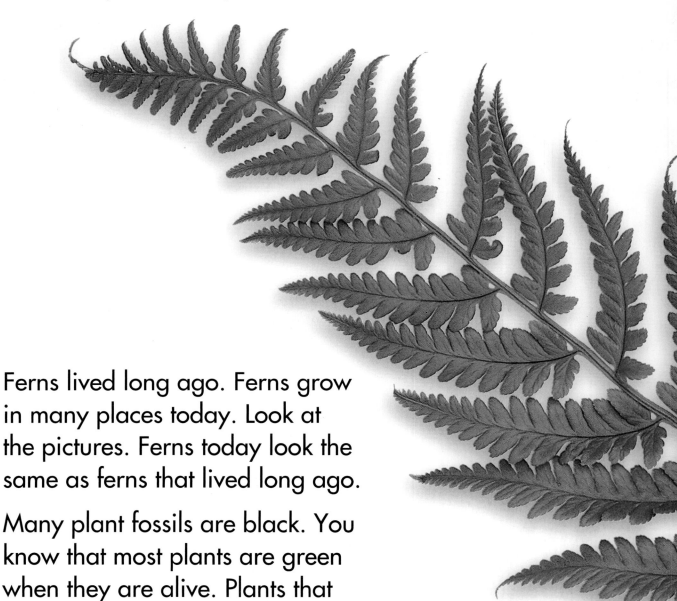

Ferns lived long ago. Ferns grow in many places today. Look at the pictures. Ferns today look the same as ferns that lived long ago.

Many plant fossils are black. You know that most plants are green when they are alive. Plants that lived long ago were probably green too.

This is how a fern looks today.

This fossil of a fern is black. It was found in a rock.

This flower lives today. It is called a primrose.

This flower fossil looks almost like a primrose!

✓ **Lesson Review**

1. Why do scientists study plant fossils?

TARGET SKILL

2. **Use Graphic Organizers** Write how plant fossils give us clues about plants from long ago. Use a graphic organizer to help you.

Measuring Fossil Leaves

Look at the fossils of 3 leaves.
Measure the leaves.

Make a bar graph like this one. Copy the title and labels. Fill in the bar for each leaf. Use your bar graph to answer the questions.

1. Which leaf is the longest?

2. Which leaf is the shortest?

3. How much longer is the longest leaf than the shortest leaf?

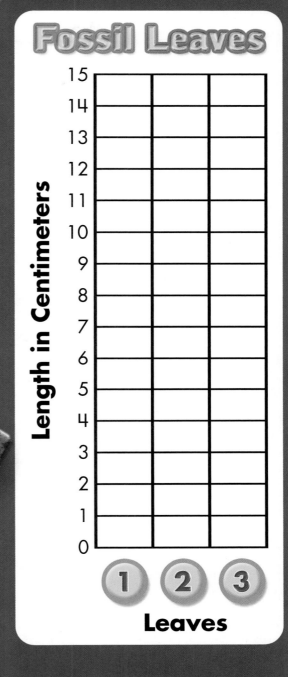

Fossil Leaves

Length in Centimeters

15 14 13 12 11 10 9 8 7 6 5 4 3 2 1 0

1 2 3

Leaves

Lab zone Take-Home Activity

Find 3 leaves in your neighborhood. Measure the leaves. Make a bar graph to show how long the leaves are.

Guided Inquiry

Investigate How can you make a model of a fossil?

Materials

shell

clay

classroom objects

metric ruler

What to Do

1 **Make a model** of a fossil. Press a shell into clay.

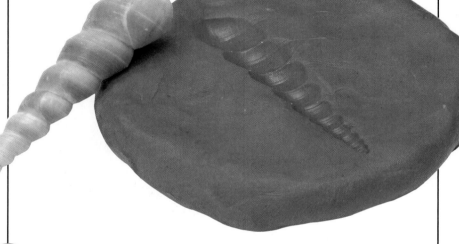

2 **Observe** the shell and the fossil. **Measure** how long they are. Use centimeters.

How are the fossil model and the shell alike and different?	
Alike	**Different**

Process Skills

You **infer** when you use what you know and **observe** to explain something.

3 Pick an object in your classroom.
Make a fossil model of the object.

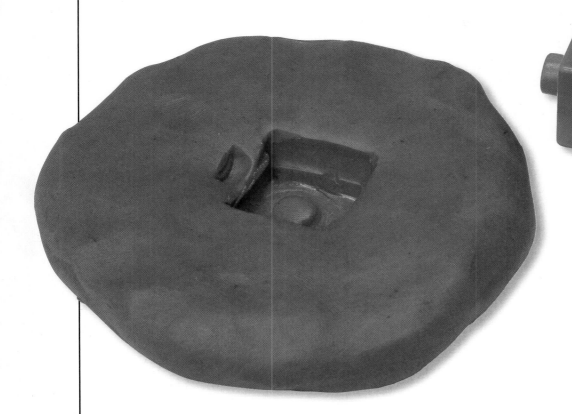

4 Trade with another sudent.
Observe the new fossil model. What is it?

Explain Your Results

1. **Infer** What was the new fossil model? How did you know?
2. How do fossils give clues about living things?

Go Further

What else could you do to make models of fossils? Make a plan and try it.

Focus on the BIG Idea People can learn about the Earth long ago by studying fossils of plants and animals.

Lesson 1

What is a fossil?

- A fossil is a print or part of a plant or animal that lived long ago.
- Fossils show the size and shape of plants and animals that lived long ago.

Lesson 2

How do we learn about life long ago?

- Scientists study fossils to help us learn about plants and animals that lived on Earth long ago.
- Scientists build skeletons from bones of animals that lived long ago.

Lesson 3

What were dinosaurs like?

- Dinosaurs were animals that lived on Earth long ago.
- Some dinosaurs ate meat using long, sharp teeth.
- Some dinosaurs ate plants using short, flat teeth.

Lesson 4

How are plants and animals of long ago like those today?

- Scientists study fossils to learn how plants and animals that lived long ago are like plants and animals today.

Cross-Curricular Links

English–Language Arts

Building Vocabulary

Look again at pages 200–201. Find the picture for the word *dinosaur*. Write a story about different types of dinosaurs. Describe how they looked and what they ate.

Mathematics

Lengths of Skeletons

A *Compsognathus* skeleton was found in France. It is 125 centimeters long. Another was found in Germany. It is 90 centimeters long. How much longer is the skeleton found in France?

Visual and Performing Arts

Drawing a Dinosaur

Find out about a type of dinosaur called a pterodactyl. Write a description of this dinosaur. Draw a picture of what you think this dinosaur looked like. Color your picture.

Challenge!

Mathematics

Measuring Length

You learned that a dinosaur called a tyrannosauroid was about 2 meters long. Measure 2 meters in your classroom. Think of some objects that are about 2 meters long.

Vocabulary

Which picture goes with each word?

1. fossil (page 205)

2. skeleton (page 208)

3. dinosaur (page 210)

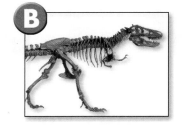

Think About It

4. Why do scientists study fossils? (pages 208—211)

5. Why do scientists study the teeth of dinosaurs? (page 216)

6. **Writing in Science** Suppose you discovered a fossil. Write a letter to a friend telling about your discovery. (pages 205—207)

7. **Process Skills** **Make and Use Models** Scientists can use what they learn from fossils to make a model of a dinosaur. How is a model like a real dinosaur? How is it different? (pages 214—215)

8. 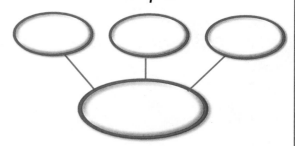 **Use Graphic Organizers**

Use a word web to write about a *Triceratops.*

(pages 203, 217)

A *Triceratops* had three horns on its head! It had a beak like a bird. A *Triceratops* ate plants using its short, flat teeth.

California Standards Practice

Write the letter of the correct answer.

9. How do scientists learn about life long ago?

  A by studying pushes and pulls

  B by studying fossils

  C by studying volume and pitch

  D by studying magnets

10. Look at the picture. What animal does this fossil look like?

  A a bear

  B a whale

  C a fish

  D a cow

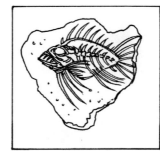

Satellites Help Scientists Find Fossils

Read Together

NASA Landsat satellites go around Earth. Landsat satellites send information about land on Earth. This information helps some scientists find places to look for fossils.

A fossil is a print or part of a plant or animal that lived long ago. Some fossils are found in rocks. Look at the pictures of fossils on the next page.

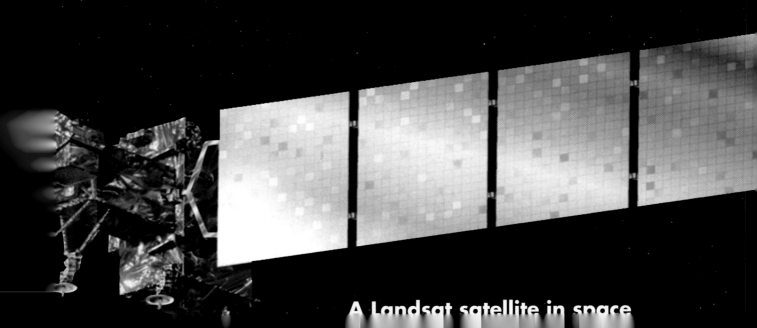

A Landsat satellite in space

Fossils can teach us about animals that lived on Earth. Fossils can teach us about Earth's past.

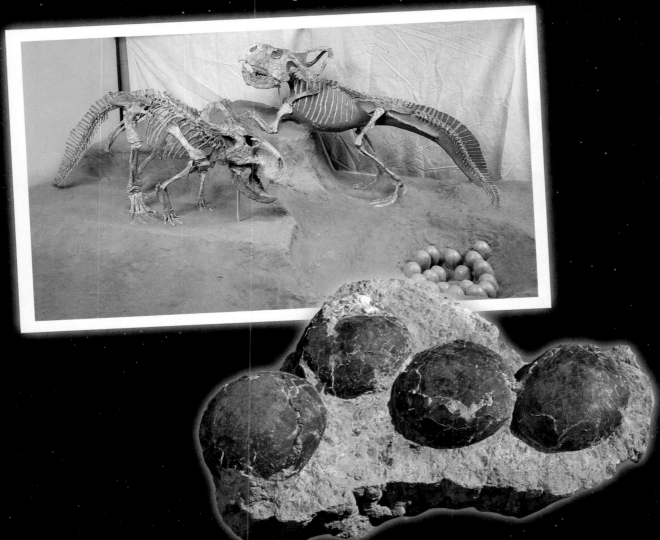

This is a fossil of dinosaur eggs.

Lab zone Take-Home Activity

Find a tree leaf. Draw what you think the fossil of the tree leaf will look like.

A *Tyrannosaurus rex* skeleton

Susan Hendrickson

Read Together

How would you like to have a dinosaur named after you? This *Tyrannosaurus rex* is named Sue. It is named after Susan Hendrickson. Susan Hendrickson looks for animals that no longer live on Earth. She wants to show them in museums.

Susan Hendrickson found the fossil bones of this *Tyrannosaurus rex.* You can see Sue the *Tyrannosaurus rex* if you visit the Field Museum in Chicago.

Sue, the *Tyrannosaurus rex* skeleton

Lab zone Take-Home Activity

Use pipe cleaners to make a model of a *Tyrannosaurus rex* skeleton. Share your model with your family.

Unit C Summary

Chapter 6

What are some of Earth's natural resources?

- Natural resources are useful materials that come from Earth.
- Soil, water, rocks, and plants are some of Earth's natural resources.

Chapter 7

How can people learn about Earth long ago?

- People can use fossils of plants and animals to learn what Earth was like long ago.

Experiment How much water do different soils hold?

In this experiment, you will study how well loam and sand hold water.

Materials

spoon

loam and sand

2 filter cups
(prepared by teacher)

water, graduated
cylinder, measuring cup

Process Skills

You **control variables** when you change only one thing in an **experiment.**

Ask a question.

Do some soils hold more water than others?

Make a hypothesis.

Will loam and sand hold different amounts of water? Tell what you think.

Plan a fair test.

Use the same amount of soil and water.

Do your test.

1. Put a filter cup in a plastic cup.

2. **Measure** 100 mL of loam with a measuring cup. Pour it into the filter cup.

Be careful!

Wash your hands after handling soils.

3 Measure 50 mL of water with a graduated cylinder. Pour it on the loam.

4 Pour the water from the plastic cup into the graduated cylinder. Measure. Record.

5 Repeat steps 1 to 4 for the sand.

Collect and record data.

Soil Type	Water Added (mL)	Water in Plastic Cup (mL)	Water Left in Soil (mL)
Loam	50 mL		
Sand	50 mL		

Tell your conclusion.
Did one soil hold more water than the other? Explain how you know.

Go Further
How well does clay soil hold water? Make and carry out a plan to find out the answer to this or another question you may have.

Make a Model

- Find a picture of your favorite dinosaur.

- Make a model of the dinosaur using clay and other classroom materials.

- Tell your group what you have learned about dinosaurs.

Write a Nonfiction Story

A nonfiction story is a piece of writing that is true. Write a nonfiction story about scientists that study dinosaurs. Tell how scientists look for fossil bones. Tell how scientists put the bones together to build a dinosaur skeleton.

Read More About Earth Sciences

Look for other books about Earth Sciences in your library-media center. One book you may want to read is:

Fossils Tell of Long Ago by Aliki

This book tells how fossils are formed and where they are found. It also shows you how to make a fossil.

Science Fair Projects

Full Inquiry

Using Scientific Methods
1. Ask a question.
2. Make a hypothesis.
3. Plan a fair test.
4. Do your test.
5. Collect and record data.
6. Tell your conclusion.
7. Go further.

Idea 1
The Best Soil for Planting

Plan a project. Find out whether one kind of plant grows best in sandy soil, clay soil, or loam.

Idea 2
A Dinosaur's Diet

Plan a project. Find out whether different kinds of dinosaurs ate plants or meat.

Unit C California Standards Practice

Write the letter of the correct answer.

1. **What is luster?**

   A the shape of a mineral
   B how hard a mineral is
   C the color of a mineral
   D how shiny or dull a mineral is

2. **What are rocks made of?**

   A weathered soil and water
   B different kinds of minerals
   C concrete and gravel
   D ice and water

3. **What happens to a big rock because of weathering?**

    A It becomes harder.

    B It stays the same.

    C It breaks down into smaller rocks.

    D It becomes larger.

4. **Which statement is true about gophers and worms?**

    A They do not like soil.

    B They stay above the ground.

    C They make the soil harder.

    D They loosen and mix the soil.

5. **Look at the picture. What is a fossil?**

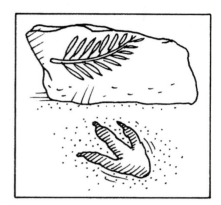

    A a young plant

    B a young animal

    C a print or part of a plant or animal that lived long ago

    D a plant or an animal that lives on Earth today

6. **How do scientists learn about life on Earth long ago?**

    A by studying what people eat

    B by studying fossils

    C by studying the weather

    D by studying the environment

Unit C California Standards Practice

7. What is one way scientists can learn about the size of a dinosaur?

A by building a skeleton of a dinosaur
B by making dinosaur footprints
C by cleaning fossil bones
D by studying dinosaurs who ate plants

8. What did dinosaurs with short, flat teeth eat?

A plants
B other animals
C meat
D rocks and soil

California Science Content Standards, Grade 2

STANDARD SET 1. Physical Sciences

2PS1.0 The motion of objects can be observed and measured. As a basis for understanding this concept:

2PS1.a Students know the position of an object can be described by locating it in relation to another object or to the background.	pp. **6,** 9, **10, 11, 32, 35, 67**
2PS1.b Students know an object's motion can be described by recording the change in position of the object over time.	pp. **12, 13,** 18, **32,** 33, 34, 35, 62, 63
2PS1.c Students know the way to change how something is moving is by giving it a push or a pull. The size of the change is related to the strength or the amount of force, of the push or pull.	pp. 8, **14, 15, 16, 18, 32,** 33, **34,** 36, 37, 61, 67, 68
2PS1.d Students know tools and machines are used to apply pushes and pulls (forces) to make things move.	pp. **18,** 19, 20, 21, 32, 34, **67**
2PS1.e Students know objects fall to the ground unless something holds them up.	pp. **22, 23,** 32, 34, 61, 69
2PS1.f Students know magnets can be used to make some objects move without being touched.	pp. **24,** 25, **26,** 27, 28, 29, 30, **31,** 32, 34, 61, **68**
2PS1.g Students know sound is made by vibrating objects and can be described by its pitch and volume.	pp. 42, 44, **45,** 46, 47, 48, 49, 50, 51, **52, 53,** 54, 55, 56, 58, 59, 61, **64,** 69, 70

What It Means to You

You can push a ball and it rolls along the floor. You can jump up but you get pulled back down again. You can pull a paper clip to a magnet, even without touching the paper clip! You can push and pull objects to make them move. You can hear sound when something vibrates. You can change the volume and pitch of sound.

California Science Content Standards, Grade 2

STANDARD SET 2. Life Sciences

2LS2.0 Plants and animals have predictable life cycles. As a basis for understanding this concept:

2LS2.a Students know that organisms reproduce offspring of their own kind and that the offspring resemble their parents and one another.	pp. 76, 78, **79,** 80, 81, **82, 83, 94,** 96, 97, 110, 112, 113, 114, 115, 116, 117, 150, **155,** 161, 162, 163
2LS2.b Students know the sequential stages of life cycles are different for different animals, such as butterflies, frogs, and mice.	pp. **102,** 104, 105, 106, 107, 108, 109, 112, 113, 114, 115, **110, 111,** 116, 117, 118, 119, **120, 121, 122, 124, 125, 155,** 162, 163
2LS2.c Students know many characteristics of an organism are inherited from the parents. Some characteristics are caused or influenced by the environment.	pp. **80,** 81, **82, 83,** 94, 96, 97, 113, **155,** 161
2LS2.d Students know there is variation among individuals of one kind within a population.	pp. **78, 79, 81,** 86, **87,** 88, **89,** 92, 93, 94, 97
2LS2.e Students know light, gravity, touch, or environmental stress can affect the germination, growth, and development of plants.	pp. 83, 84, 85, 94, 96, 98, 132, 134, 135, **136, 137, 138, 139,** 140, 141, 146, 147, 148, 149, **150,** 152, 153, 155, 156, 157, 161, 163, 164
2LS2.f Students know flowers and fruits are associated with reproduction in plants.	pp. **142, 143, 144, 145, 150,** 152, 153, 155, 158, 164

What It Means to You

Young plants and animals look like their parents in some ways, but look different in other ways. Changes in the world around us can change the way some plants and animals look and grow. Some animals change as they grow. Plants grow and change too.

California Science Content Standards, Grade 2

STANDARD SET 3. Earth Sciences

2ES3.0 Earth is made of materials that have distinct properties and provide resources for human activities. As the basis for understanding this concept:

2ES3.a Students know how to compare the physical properties of different kinds of rocks and know that rock is composed of different combinations of minerals.	pp. 170, 171, 173, 174, 175, 176, 177, 190, 191, **192, 193, 194,** 196, 198, 239
2ES3.b Students know smaller rocks come from the breakage and weathering of larger rocks.	pp. **178,** 179, **180,** 181, **194,** 196, 197, 239, 240
2ES3.c Students know that soil is made partly from weathered rock and partly from organic materials and that soils differ in their color, texture, capacity to retain water, and ability to support the growth of many kinds of plants.	pp. **182, 183, 184, 185,** 187, **194,** 197, 234, 235, 240
2ES3.d Students know that fossils provide evidence about the plants and animals that lived long ago and that scientists learn about the past history of Earth by studying fossils.	pp. 166, 202, 204, **205, 206,** 207, 208, 209, 210, 211, 212, 214, 215, 216, 217, 218, 219, 220, 221, 222, 223, 224, 225, **226,** 228, 229, 232, 233, 236, 241, 242
2ES3.e Students know rock, water, plants, and soil provide many resources, including food, fuel, and building materials, that humans use.	pp. 171, **186, 187, 188, 189, 194,** 196, **233**

What It Means to You

Rocks are made up of different kinds of minerals. You know about some of the minerals that come from Earth. Some of these minerals are hard, some are soft, some are dull, and some are shiny. You know that weathering can change the way some rocks look. You know about some of Earth's natural resources and how people use them. What was Earth like when dinosaurs were living on Earth? You know about fossils and the clues they show about plants and animals that lived a very long time ago.

California Science Content Standards, Grade 2

STANDARD SET 4. Investigation and Experimentation

2IE4.0 Scientific progress is made by asking meaningful questions and conducting careful investigations. As a basis for understanding this concept and addressing the content in the other three strands, students should develop their own questions and perform investigations. Students will:

2IE4.a Make predictions based on observed patterns and not random guessing.	pp. **30, 31, 42, 54, 55, 62, 63,**
2IE4.b Measure length, weight, temperature, and liquid volume with appropriate tools and express those measurements in standard metric system units.	pp. **62, 63, 92,** 93, 148, 149, 156, **157, 170, 224,** 225, **234, 235**
2IE4.c Compare and sort common objects according to two or more physical attributes (e.g., color, shape, texture, size, weight).	pp. 76, 92, 93, **170, 192, 193**
2IE4.d Write or draw descriptions of a sequence of steps, events, and observations.	pp. 102, **120, 121, 132, 202, 224, 225**
2IE4.e Construct bar graphs to record data, using appropriately labeled axes.	pp. **92, 93, 157**
2IE4.f Use magnifiers or microscopes to observe and draw descriptions of small objects or small features of objects.	pp. **92, 102, 120, 121, 149, 192, 193**
2IE4.g Follow oral instructions for a scientific investigation.	p. **6**

What It Means to You

Investigations help you answer questions. They help you predict. You know that patterns help you predict too. You know to follow what your teacher tells you when you investigate. Tools help you measure. You can compare and sort objects by properties. Drawing or writing helps you remember what you learn. A magnifier or a microscope helps you look closer at things. You might use a bar graph to show what you learn.

Glossary

The glossary uses letters and signs to show how words are pronounced. The mark ′ is placed after a syllable with a primary or heavy accent. The mark ′ is placed after a syllable with a secondary or lighter accent.

To hear these words pronounced, listen to the AudioText CD.

A

amphibian (am fib′ē ən) An animal that lives part of its life in water and part on land. A toad is an **amphibian.** (page 107)

answer questions (an′sər kwes′chənz) Give a response when you are asked something. I can **answer questions** as I read. (page 43)

ask questions (ask kwes′chənz) What you do to find out something. I **ask questions** about what I am reading. (page 43)

attract (ə trakt′) Pull toward. The opposite poles of two magnets **attract** one another. (page 24)

background (bak′ground′) The position behind an object. The trees are in the **background** of the soccer game. (page 10)

caterpillar (kat′ər pil′ər) The larva stage of a butterfly. A **caterpillar** is long and fuzzy. (page 114)

cause (kȯz) Why something happens. Taking out the bottom block can be the **cause** of the tower falling. (page 7)

classify (klas′ə fī) To put things that are alike in groups. You can **classify** rocks. (page xii)

collect data (kə lekt′ dā′tə)
To gather information. You can
collect data by measuring
things. (page 62)

communicate (kə myü′nə kāt)
To use words or pictures to share
information. I **communicate** by
drawing a picture. (page xv)

control variables (kən trōl′ vâr′ē
ə bəlz) To change only one thing
in a fair test. Scientists **control
variables.** (page xv)

details (di tālz′) Pieces of
information that tell you about
something. We looked for
important **details** in the book.
(page 133)

dinosaur (dī′nə sôr) Animal that
lived on Earth long ago. Some
dinosaurs ate plants.
(page 210)

draw conclusions (drȯ kən klü′zhənz) To decide something about what you see or read. You can **draw** a **conclusion** about what the shark will eat. (page 171)

effect (ə fekt′) What happens. The **effect** of pulling out the bottom block was that the blocks fell down. (page 7)

environment (en vī′rən mənt) Everything around a living thing like air, sunlight, water, and soil. A lily will have many flowers in a sunny **environment.** (page 84)

experiment (ek sper′ə ment) To use scientific methods to test a hypothesis. You can **experiment** with plants. (page 62)

F

fair test (fâr test) To make sure only one thing is changed in an experiment. The experiment was a **fair test** because only the temperature was changed. (page 62)

force (fôrs) A push or a pull that makes something move. The children used **force** to play soccer. (page 14)

fossil (fos′əl) A print or part of a plant or animal that lived long ago. **Fossils** help us learn about animals that lived long ago. (page 205)

friction (frik′shən) A force that makes a moving object slow down or stop moving. **Friction** causes the bicycle to slow down. (page 16)

fuel (fyü′əl) Anything that is burned to make heat or power. We use gasoline as **fuel** for our car. (page 189)

germinate (jėr′mə nāt) Begin to grow. A seed that has enough water and air may **germinate.** (page 144)

granite (gran′it) A type of rock with large grains of minerals. **Granite** is used in buildings. (page 174)

graphic organizer (graf′ik ôr′gə nīz ər) A drawing that shows the relationships between words. The **graphic organizer** shows the main idea and details of the paragraph. (page 203)

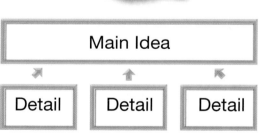

Main Idea

| Detail | Detail | Detail |

gravity (grav′ə tē) A force that pulls things toward the center of Earth. If I drop a toy, **gravity** will pull it down to Earth. (page 22)

hypothesis (hī poth′ə sis) A statement of one possible way to answer a question. My experiment proved that my **hypothesis** was right. (page 62)

infer (in fėr′) To make a guess based on what you have learned or what you know. I can **infer** from my test that loam holds water better than sandy soil. (page 102)

inherit (in her′it) To get some things from one's parents. The bunny will **inherit** its parents' long ears. (page 80)

insect (in′sekt) An animal that has three body parts and six legs. A dragonfly is an **insect.**
(page 106)

interpret data (in tėr′prit dā′tə) Using the information collected to answer questions. I can **interpret** the **data** shown in the graph.
(page 92)

investigate (in ves′tə gāt) Solve a problem or answer a question by following steps. You can **investigate** to see if a certain plant needs more sunlight.
(page 30)

larva (lär′və) a young insect. A caterpillar is a butterfly **larva.**
(page 114)

life cycle (līf sī′kəl) The way a living thing grows and changes. Frogs have a **life cycle.** (page 105)

luster (lus′tər) How shiny or dull a mineral is. Azurite is a mineral that has a shiny **luster.** (page 177)

machine (mə shēn′) An object that makes it easier to move things. A wagon is a **machine.** (page 21)

magnet (mag′nit) An object that can pull some kinds of metal objects. The **magnet** attracts the paper clips. (page 24)

main idea (mān ī dē′ ə) The most important idea in a passage. The **main idea** of my paper is that fossils teach us about the past. (page 133)

mammal (mam′əl) An animal that usually has hair or fur on its body. Young **mammals** look like their parents. (page 106)

minerals (min′ər əlz) Nonliving materials that come from Earth. Silver is a **mineral.** (page 174)

model (mod′l) A drawing or object that represents something else. Our class has a **model** of the solar system. (page 224)

motion (mō′shən) The act of moving. The speed and direction of **motion** can be changed. (page 12)

natural resource (nach′ər əl rē′sôrs) A useful material that comes from Earth. Water is a **natural resource.** (page 186)

nutrient (nü′trē ənt) Something that living things need to live and grow. Plants get **nutrients** from the soil. (page 135)

nymph (nimf) The second stage in the life cycle of some insects. A grasshopper **nymph** has no wings. (page 116)

observe (əb zėrv′) To use your senses to find out about things. Scientists **observe** fossils. (page 171)

offspring (ȯf′spring′) Young plants and animals. Some **offspring** look like their parents. (page 79)

pitch (pich) How high or low a sound is. A triangle makes a sound with a high **pitch.** (page 50)

pollen (pol′ən) A powder found in flowers. **Pollen** is needed to make seeds grow. (page 142)

position (pə zish′ən) Where an object is. Words such as *in front of* and *behind* can help you describe **position**. (page 9)

predict (pri dikt′) To make a guess about what will happen from what you already know. I **predict** the magnet will pull the spoon. (page 30)

pupa (pyü′pə) The stage after the larva in the life cycle of some insects. A hard covering protects the **pupa** of the butterfly. (page 114)

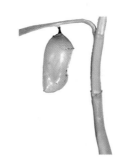

purpose (pėr′pəs) The reason for something. I can state the **purpose** of a story. (page 103)

R

repel (ri pel′) Push away. Like poles of two magnets will **repel** each other. (page 24)

rock (rok) The hard, solid part of the Earth that is not soil or metal. **Rocks** can come in different colors. (page 173)

root (rüt) The part of a plant that holds the plant in place and takes in water and nutrients from the soil. **Roots** grow down into the soil. (page 136)

S

scientific methods (sī′ən tif′ik meth′ədz) A way of finding answers and solving problems. I can use **scientific methods** to find out how light affects plants. (page xvi)

seed (sēd) The part of a plant that has a tiny new plant inside it. I planted the **seeds** in the garden. (page 142)

seed coat (sēd kōt) The hard outer covering of a seed. The **seed coat** protects the new plant. (page 143)

seedling (sēd′ling) A young plant. A peach **seedling** grows into a peach tree. (page 144)

skeleton (skel′ə tən) All of the bones of a body. Scientists put together the **skeletons** of dinosaurs. (page 208).

soil (soil) The top layer of Earth. Loam is a **soil** that holds water well. (page 182)

stage (stāj) A part of the life cycle of an animal. A butterfly has four **stages** in its life cycle. (page 105)

stem (stem) The part of a plant that holds it up and carries water and nutrients to the leaves. Some flowers have long **stems.** (page 136)

 T

tadpole (tad′pōl) The second stage of a frog's life cycle. A **tadpole** has a tail. (page 108)

text features (tekst fē′ chərz) Things that show how a book is organized. The table of contents is a **text feature.** (page 77)

 V

vibrate (vī′brāt) Move quickly back and forth. Parts of your throat **vibrate** when you talk. (page 45)

volume (vol′yəm) How loud or soft a sound is. The **volume** of the sounds this animal makes is loud. (page 48)

weathering (weᴛʜ′ər ing) The breaking apart and changing of rocks. **Weathering** caused a big rock to break apart into smaller rocks. (page 178)

weight (wāt) A measure of the pull of gravity on an object. You can find the **weight** of an object by measuring how heavy it is. (page 23)

Index

This Index lists the pages on which topics appear in this book. Page numbers after a *p* refer to a photograph. Page numbers after a *c* refer to a chart or graph.

Credits

Illustrations

10, 12 Matt Zang; 35, 59, 69, 125, 153, 161, 197, 229, 241 Kathie Kelleher; 185, 193, 199–200, 203, 210, 212, 226, 233, 238 Big Sesh Studios; 203 Alan Barnard

Photographs

Every effort has been made to secure permission and provide appropriate credit for photographic material. The publisher deeply regrets any omission and pledges to correct errors called to its attention in subsequent editions.

Unless otherwise acknowledged, all photographs are the property of Scott Foresman, a division of Pearson Education.

Photo locators denoted as follows: Top (T), Center (C), Bottom (B), Left (L), Right (R), Background (Bkgd).

Cover: (L) ©Flip Nicklin/Minden Pictures, (R) ©Norbert Wu/Minden Pictures, (C) ©Hiroya Minakuchi/Minden Pictures

Front Matter: vi ©ThinkStock/SuperStock; vii (T) Getty Images, (B) ©DK Images; viii (T) Getty Images, (B) ©Ingo Arndt/Nature Picture Library; ix (T) Corbis, (B) Jupiter Images; x (T) ©Craig Aurness/Corbis, (B) ©Lester Lefkowitz/Corbis; xii ©Reuters/Corbis; xiii (BR) Corbis, (CR) Harry Taylor/Courtesy of the Natural History Museum, London/©DK Images; xiv (Bkgd) ©Stuart Westmorland/Corbis, (R) ©DK Limited/Corbis, (B) Andy Crawford/Courtesy of the Senckenberg Nature Museum, Frankfurt/©DK Images; xvi ©blickwinkel/Alamy Images; xix ©Royalty-Free/Corbis

Unit A – Opener: 1 ©Michael Dunning/Getty Images; 2 ©Jurgen Vogt/Getty Images; 3 ©Dennis Kitchen/Getty Images; 4 (Bkgd) ©Paul Barton/Corbis, (BR) ©ThinkStock/SuperStock; 7 (TR) ©Taxi/Getty Images, (TR) ©Photographer's Choice/Getty Images, (CL) ©Emely/zefa/Corbis, (Bkgd) ©Paul Barton/Corbis; 8 ©Paul Barton/Corbis; 9 Getty Images; 14 (TL) Hemera Technologies, (L) ©Chapman/NewSport/Corbis; 15 ©AFP/Getty Images; 16 Hemera Technologies; 17 (T) ©Mike Brinson/Getty Images, (B) ©ThinkStock/SuperStock; 18 (BL) ©Nation Wong/Corbis, (R) ©Lester Lefkowitz/Corbis, (C) ©Donald Miralle/Getty Images; 19 ©Tim Boyle/Getty Images; 20 Hemera Technologies; 22 ©Chris Carroll/Corbis; 26 Hemera Technologies; 32 (Bkgd) Getty Images, (TL) ©Paul Barton/Corbis, (CL) ©Mike Brinson/Getty Images, (CL) ©Nation Wong/Corbis, (BL) ©Chris Carroll/Corbis; 34 (CL) ©Paul Barton/Corbis, (CR) ©ThinkStock/SuperStock; 36 (B) ©Johnson Space Center/NASA, (Bkgd) NASA; 37 GRIN/NASA Image Exchange; 38 (Bkgd) Corbis, (TL) ©Jeff Caplan/Langley Research Center/NASA; 39 ©Ariel Skelley/Corbis; 40 (B) ©Kevin Schafer/Corbis, (T) Getty Images; 41 Dave King/©DK Images; 43 (Bkgd, TR, CL) Getty Images; 44 Getty Images; 45 (TR) Dave King/©DK Images, (BR) ©DK Images; 46 ©Image Quest 3-D/NHPA Limited; 47 ©James H. Robinson/Photo Researchers, Inc.; 48 (TL) Hemera Technologies, (CR) ©Jeff Hunter/Getty Images, (BL) ©Walter Hodges/Corbis, (BR) ©George Hall/Corbis, (CL) ©Kevin Schafer/Corbis; 49 (BL) Getty Images, (TR, BR) ©Royalty-Free/Corbis, (TL) ©The Image Bank/Getty Images; 50 Dave King/©DK Images; 52 ©Tom Tracy/Corbis; 56 (Bkgd) ©James Noble/Corbis, (TL) Getty Images, (TL) ©Kevin Schafer/Corbis, (TL) Dave King/©DK Images; 60 (Bkgd) ©Royalty-Free/Corbis, (Bkgd) ©S. Maka/Corbis, (TR) ©Alejandro Purgue; 61 (TL) ©Dennis Kitchen/Getty Images, (B) ©Jurgen Vogt/Getty Images, (CL) ©Ariel Skelley/Corbis; 65 Getty Images; 66 (B, Bkgd) Getty Images; 67 ©Michael Boys/Corbis; **Unit B – Opener:** 71 (Bkgd) ©Brandon Harman/Getty Images, (C) ©Cyril Laubscher/Getty Images; 72 (CR) ©Tim Fitzharris/Minden Pictures, (Bkgd) ©Anthony Arendt/Ambient Images, Inc.; 73 (Bkgd) Getty Images, (C) ©Stephen Dalton/Photo Researchers, Inc.; 74 (BL) Getty Images, (Bkgd) ©Royalty-Free/Corbis, (Bkgd) ©Kathryn Russell/Jupiter Images, (BR) ©Tania Midgley/Corbis; 75 (BR, BL) ©GK & Vikki Hart/Getty Images; 77 (Bkgd) ©Kathryn Russell/Jupiter Images, (Bkgd) ©Royalty-Free/Corbis, (TR) ©Stephen Dalton/Photo Researchers, Inc.; 78 (B) ©Royalty-Free/Corbis, (TL) Clive Boursnell/©DK Images, (Bkgd) ©Kathryn Russell/Jupiter Images; 79 (TR, CL) Getty Images; 80 (B) ©GK & Vikki Hart/Getty Images, (TL) ©DK Images; 81 (TL, TR) Jane Burton/©DK Images, (B) ©GK & Vikki Hart/Getty Images, (TR) ©DK Images; 82 (R) ©Robert Landau/Corbis, (BL) ©Taxi/Getty Images, (TL) Jupiter Images; 83 ©DK Images; 84 ©Tania Midgley/Corbis, (TL, R, BL) Getty Images; 86 (TL) Clive Boursnell/©DK Images, (BL) ©Michael Boys/Corbis, (C) Colin Walton/©DK Images; 87 Clive Boursnell/©DK Images; 88 ©American Images Inc./Getty Images; 89 (BR) Dave King/©DK Images, (TR) ©DK Images; 90 (CL) ©Hans Strand/Getty Images, (CR) ©Dave King/Getty Images, (L) ©Carol Polich/Getty Images, (R) ©Bob Elsdale/Getty Images; 93 (TR) ©DK Images, (CR) ©Michael and Patricia Fogden/Corbis; 94 (TL) ©Kathryn Russell/Jupiter Images, (TL) ©Royalty-Free/Corbis, (Bkgd) ©Stuart Westmorland/Corbis, (TL) ©D. Robert & Lorri Franz/Corbis, (CL) ©Michael Boys/Corbis, (BL) ©American Images Inc./Getty Images, (BR) ©DK Images; 96 (TR) Jane Burton/©DK Images, (TL) ©Tania Midgley/Corbis, (CR, BR) ©American Images Inc./Getty Images; 98 (B) ©Kevin Cruff/Getty Images, (TL) ©CMSP/Getty Images, (CL) Getty Images, (CL) Digital Vision; 99 (Bkgd) ©Johnny Johnson/Getty Images, (TL) ©Ken Graham/Getty Images; 100 (TL, B, BR) ©DK Images, (BR) ©Johnny Johnson/Getty Images, (BL) ©Ingo Arndt/Nature Picture Library; 101 (BL, TL) ©DK Images, (CR) ©Michael and Patricia Fogden/Corbis, (BR) ©George D. Lepp/Corbis; 102 (T) ©Gladden William Willis/Animals Animals/Earth Scenes, (TR, TC) ©T. Kitchin & V. Hurst/NHPA Limited, (TCR) ©Stephen Dalton/NHPA Limited, (TR, CR, BR) ©DK Images; 103 (Bkgd) ©Stephen Dalton/NHPA Limited, (CR) ©DK Images; 106 (TL) Courtesy of Digital Dragonflies, (BR) ©DK Images, (TR) ©Johnny Johnson/Getty Images; 107 (TL) ©Fabio Liverani/Nature Picture Library, (TR) ©Ingo Arndt/Nature Picture Library; 108 (B, CL, TL, TCL) ©DK Images; 109 ©DK Images; 110 (B, C, T) ©DK Images; 111 ©DK Images; 112 (BL, CR) Kim Taylor/©DK Images; 113 Kim Taylor/©DK Images; 114 (B) ©Michael and Patricia Fogden/Corbis, (TR) ©George D. Lepp/Corbis; 115 (T) ©DK Images, (B) ©George D. Lepp/Corbis; 116 (TL, B) ©R. Al Simpson/Visuals Unlimited, (TR) ©Raymond Mendez/Animals Animals/Earth Scenes; 117 ©Patti Murray/Animals Animals/Earth Scenes; 118 (C) ©Michael Newman/PhotoEdit, (C) ©Robert Pickett/Corbis, (C) ©Richard Shiell/Animals Animals/Earth Scenes, (C) ©Kevin Schafer/Corbis, (Bkgd) ©The Image Bank/Getty Images; 120 Courtesy of the Winnipeg Cereal Research Center, Winnipeg, Canada; 122 (Bkgd) ©Art Wolfe/Getty Images, (TL) ©Stephen Dalton/NHPA Limited, (TL) ©DK Images, (CL) Kim Taylor/©DK Images, (BL) ©Michael and Patricia Fogden/Corbis, (CL) ©R. Al Simpson/Visuals Unlimited, (BR) ©Patti Murray/Animals Animals/Earth Scenes; 124 (BL) ©Ingo Arndt/Nature Picture Library, (TR, CL) ©DK Images, (TC) ©Johnny Johnson/Getty Images, (CR) ©George D. Lepp/Corbis, (BL) ©Michael and Patricia Fogden/Corbis; 125 Kim Taylor/©DK Images; 126 NASA; 127 (TR) ©Photolink/Getty Images, (CL) ©Porterfield/Chickering/Photo Researchers, Inc., (BR) ©Doug Perrine/DRK Photo; 128 (Bkgd) ©Fred Bruemmer/DRK Photo, (T) ©Carl & Ann Purcell/Corbis, (CL) NASA; 129 (BL) Getty Images, (Bkgd) ©Sylvia Duran Sharnoff/Getty Images; 130 (BL) Getty Images, (T) Corbis; 131 ©Jerome Wexler/Visuals Unlimited; 133 (CR) ©Phillip Schermeister/Getty Images, (CR) ©Jonathan Nourok/Getty Images, (Bkgd) Corbis; 134 Corbis; 135 Jupiter Images; 136 (C, B, TL) ©DK Images; 137 ©M. T. Frazier/Photo Researchers, Inc.; 138 (TL) Hemera Technologies, (R) ©Holt Studios International Ltd/Alamy Images, (BL) ©Inga Spence/Visuals Unlimited; 139 ©Dick Makin/Alamy Images; 140 (R) ©Dr. John D. Cunningham/Visuals Unlimited, (TL) Getty Images; 141 ©LWA-JDC/Corbis; 142 Getty Images; 143 Getty Images; 144 (TR, TL) ©DK Images, (BL) ©Jerome Wexler/Visuals Unlimited, (TL) Getty Images; 145 (BR) ©Inga Spence/Visuals Unlimited, (T) ©Bill Beatty/Visuals Unlimited; 146 (T) ©Dennis MacDonald/PhotoEdit, (C) ©Inga Spence/Visuals Unlimited, (C) ©Steven Emery/Index Stock Imagery, (BR) ©Kazuko Kimizuka/Getty Images; 150 (TL, Bkgd) Corbis, (TL) ©Dick Makin/Alamy Images, (CL) ©DK Images, (BR) ©LWA-JDC/Corbis; 152 (CR) Getty Images, (TL) ©Jerome Wexler/Visuals Unlimited; 153 ©Marli Bryant Miller; 154 (B) Getty Images, (L) Hunt Institute for Botanical Documentation/Carnegie Mellon University, Pittsburgh, PA; 155 (TL) Getty Images, (B) ©Anthony Arendt/Ambient Images, Inc., (CL) ©Johnny Johnson/Getty Images, (BL) ©Sylvia Duran Sharnoff/Getty Images; 158 (T) Corbis, (B) ©Gay Bumgarner/Getty Images; 159 ©DAJ/Getty Images; 160 (B) Getty Images, (BR) ©Breck P. Kent/Animals Animals/Earth Scenes, (Bkgd) ©Stone/Getty Images; 164 ©DK Images; **Unit C – Opener:** 165 ©Jonathan Blair/Getty Images; 166 (B) ©C. Moore/Corbis, (Bkgd) ©Vanessa Berberian/Getty Images; 167 ©Royalty-Free/Corbis; 168 (T) ©Theo Allofs/zefa/Corbis, (B) ©Lester Lefkowitz/Corbis; 169 (CR) Clive Streeter/©DK Images, ©Joe McDonald/Animals Animals/Earth Scenes, (BR) ©JLP/Deimos/Corbis, (TR) Harry Taylor/©DK Images, (BL) ©Craig Aurness/Corbis; 171 (Bkgd) ©Theo Allofs/zefa/Corbis, (CR) ©Sheila Terry/Photo Researchers, Inc.; 172 ©Theo Allofs/zefa/Corbis; 173 (BR, CR) Harry Taylor/©DK Images; 174 (CL, B) ©DK Images; 175 (TL, CR, BR) ©DK Images; 176 (TCL) Harry Taylor/Courtesy of the Natural History Museum, London/©DK Images, (CR, B) Harry Taylor/©DK Images, (CL) ©Jeff Scovil; 177 Harry Taylor/©DK Images; 179 (CR) ©Fred Whitehead/Animals Animals/Earth Scenes, (TR) ©Larry Stepanowicz/Visuals Unlimited; 180 (TL, CR) ©Lester Lefkowitz/Corbis, (CL) Francesca Yorke/©DK Images; 185 ©DK Images; 186 (CL) ©The Image Bank/Getty Images, (BR) Getty Images, (CR) ©Rob Blakers/Photo Library; 187 (CR) ©Craig Aurness/Corbis, (CL) ©Inga Spence/Visuals Unlimited, (BL) Corbis, (BR) ©Ryan McVay/Getty Images; 188 (TL, R) ©Swerve/Alamy Images, (CL) ©oote boe/Alamy Images; 189 ©JLP/Deimos/Corbis; 190 (L) ©Yano Tea/Getty Images, (Bkgd) ©Richard Price/Getty Images; 191 Getty Images; 192 (CL) Harry Taylor/Courtesy of the Royal Museum of Scotland, Edinburgh/©DK Images, (BL) Colin Keates/Courtesy of the Natural History Museum, London/©DK Images, (R) ©DK Images, (TL) Tim Ridley/©DK Images; 193 ©DK Images; 194 (Bkgd) ©Image Source/Getty Images, (TL) ©Theo Allofs/zefa/Corbis, (CL) ©Larry Stepanowicz/Visuals Unlimited, (BL) ©Rob Blakers/Photo Library, (BR) Harry Taylor/©DK Images, (CL) Clive Streeter/©DK Images; 196 (BL) ©DK Images, (TL) ©Theo Allofs/zefa/Corbis, (CR) ©Larry Stepanowicz/Visuals Unlimited, (TR) ©JLP/Deimos/Corbis; 198 (Bkgd) ©Carol Polich/Getty Images, (BC) ©Ann Hagen Smith/Omni Photo Communications; 200 Colin Keates/©DK Images; 201 ©DK Images; 202 (TR) ©DK Images, (TC) Giuliano Fornari/©DK Images, (TL) Natural History Museum/©DK Images; 205 (T) Natural History Museum/©DK Images, (B) Colin Keates/©DK Images; 206 Neil Fletcher and Matthew Ward/©DK Images; 208 (CL) ©Xinhua Photo/Corbis, (BL) ©Reuters/Corbis, (TL) ©DK Images; 209 ©DK Images; 212 American Museum of Natural History; 214 (TL, C, B) Andy Crawford/©DK Images, (BL) Colin Keates/©DK Images; 216 (BL) Dave King/©DK Images, (C) GEO86284c/©The Field Museum of Natural History, Chicago; 217 Colin Keates/©DK Images; 218 (Bkgd) Getty Images, (BR) ©Steve Kaufman/Corbis, (BL) Colin Keates/©DK Images; 220 (TL) Neil Fletcher/©DK Images, (Bkgd) ©Joy Spurr/Bruce Coleman Inc.; 221 (CR) ©Barbara Strnadova/Photo Researchers, Inc., (TR) Neil Fletcher/©DK Images, (BR) ©Joy Spurr/Bruce Coleman Inc.; 222 (Bkgd) ©Pat O'Hara/Corbis, (CL, C) ©James L. Amos/Corbis, (CL) ©George H. H. Huey/Corbis, (B) Colin Keates/Courtesy of the Natural History Museum, London/©DK Images; 223 ©Lowell Georgia/Corbis; 226 (Bkgd) Getty Images, (TL) ©DK Images, (TL) ©Reuters/Corbis, (BL) ©Joy Spurr/Bruce Coleman Inc.; 228 (CL) ©Joy Spurr/Bruce Coleman Inc., (TR) ©DK Images; 230 NASA; 231 (T) ©DK Images, (C) ©Francois Gohier/Photo Researchers, Inc.; 232 (B) ©David Muench/Corbis, (BL) ©Peter Larson/Courtesy of the Black Hills Institute of Geological Research, Inc., Hill City, SD/Black Hills Institute, (CR) ©Philip Gould/Corbis, (T) ©Andy Crawford/Courtesy of the Senckenberg Nature Museum, Frankfurt/©DK Images; 233 (TL) ©Royalty-Free/Corbis, (B) ©C. Moore/Corbis; 236 (R) Getty Images, (C, T) ©Gary Ombler/Getty Images; 238 (BL) ©DK Images, (Bkgd) ©Seizo Terasaki/Getty Images, (Inset) ©Wally Eberhart/Visuals Unlimited

End Matter: EM5 ©Ingo Arndt/Nature Picture Library; EM6 ©Michael and Patricia Fogden/Corbis; EM8 Getty Images; EM9 (TR) ©AFP/Getty Images, (TL) ©Chapman/NewSport/Corbis, (B) ©ThinkStock/SuperStock, (CR) Colin Keates/©DK Images; EM10 (B) ©DK Images, (T) ©JLP/Deimos/Corbis; EM11 (B, BC) ©GK & Vikki Hart/Getty Images; EM12 (T) ©DK Images, (B) ©Michael and Patricia Fogden/Corbis; EM13 (TL, TR, CL, T) ©DK Images; EM14 (B) ©Lester Lefkowitz/Corbis, (T) ©Johnny Johnson/Getty Images, (TC) ©DK Images; EM15 (T) ©LWA-JDC/Corbis, (TC) ©R. Al Simpson/Visuals Unlimited; EM16 (B) ©George D. Lepp/Corbis, (T) Getty Images; EM17 ©Theo Allofs/zefa/Corbis; EM18 (TC, C, B) ©DK Images, (TCC) ©Jerome Wexler/Visuals Unlimited; EM19 ©DK Images

End Sheets: (C) ©Norbert Wu/Minden Pictures, (Bkgd) ©Ralph A. Clevenger/Corbis